# English Unlimited

## B2

### Self-study Pack (Workbook with DVD-ROM)

Rob Metcalf, Chris Cavey & Alison Greenwood

CAMBRIDGE UNIVERSITY PRESS
Cambridge, New York, Melbourne, Madrid, Cape Town, Singapore,
São Paulo, Delhi, Dubai, Tokyo, Mexico City

Cambridge University Press
The Edinburgh Building, Cambridge CB2 8RU, UK

www.cambridge.org
Information on this title: www.cambridge.org/9780521169714

First published 2011

Printed in the United Kingdom at the University Press, Cambridge

*A catalogue record for this publication is available from the British Library*

ISBN 978-0-521-16971-4 Upper Intermediate Self-study Pack (Workbook and DVD-ROM)
ISBN 978-0-521-73991-7 Upper Intermediate Coursebook with e-Portfolio
ISBN 978-0-521-15170-2 Upper Intermediate Teacher's Pack
ISBN 978-0-521-73992-4 Upper Intermediate Class Audio CDs

Cambridge University Press has no responsibility for the persistence or
accuracy of URLs for external or third-party internet websites referred to in
this publication, and does not guarantee that any content on such websites is,
or will remain, accurate or appropriate. Information regarding prices, travel
timetables and other factual information given in this work is correct at
the time of first printing but Cambridge University Press does not guarantee
the accuracy of such information thereafter.

# Contents

**Pull-out answer key: pages i–viii, between pages 42 and 43**

# 1 Talented

**1** Complete the welcome speech at a music academy using the words in the box.

a lot of practice   experience   feedback   results   self-esteem
specific goals   ~~talent~~   the will to succeed   training   your interests

Hello, and welcome to the Munro Academy. If you're here today, we know you possess ¹___*talent*___. But apart from having a natural ability, we know you're also confident young people who have high ²_____. You also know it's important to put in ³_____ – hours of it, every day. You're able to do this because you love playing, and decided to follow ⁴_____ from an early age. But are you also ambitious? Few people become successful musicians. Do you have ⁵_____?

If the answer is yes, then you will receive ⁶_____ of the highest quality with our teachers. This will partly focus on improving your playing. Your teachers will set ⁷_____ – things you need to achieve – and you will get immediate ⁸_____ so that you know if you're achieving them. This will help you to concentrate on ⁹_____ and not just on your technique. But another important part of your tuition will involve preparing for and giving concerts. This way, you'll build up ¹⁰_____ of performing in public.

VOCABULARY

Reacting to ideas

**2** Amy and Bill are talking about learning things when you are a child. Complete the words in their conversation.

AMY   Have you read this article? It says you learn things better when you're a young child.

BILL   That's [1]ob _vious_____.

AMY   It's not [2]sa_____ an_____ ne_____, I agree. But it explains *why*. Apparently, when you learn something later, changes happen in a different part of your brain.

BILL   That sounds [3]lo_____.

AMY   Yes, it [4]ma_____ a lot of se_____, doesn't it? The conclusion is that if you don't start young enough, you can never be as good as someone who started very young.

BILL   I'm not really [5]co_____ about that.

AMY   I don't find it very [6]pe_____ either. The scientific explanation's a bit [7]ha_____ to fo_____ too. I [8]do_____ ge_____ this bit about brain scans. I think it's saying that if you start later, the part of your brain that you use can't get very big, and that's why people who start young are always better at things.

BILL   That seems quite [9]si_____ to me. I'm sure the full explanation's more complicated.

AMY   I agree. I mean, Joseph Conrad was one of the greatest writers in English, and he couldn't speak a word of English until he was twenty-one! So it's clearly not the [10]wh_____ pi_____.

GRAMMAR

Present perfect simple and progressive

**3** Complete Sasha's email using the present perfect simple or progressive form of the verbs in brackets. Both forms may be possible.

Delete   Reply   Reply All   Forward   Print

Dear Akila

It was good talking to you after the meeting, and I'm glad you've got in touch. You ask how I learned to speak so many languages. I [1]*'ve always been* (always / be) good at languages, perhaps because of my home situation. My father's Japanese and my mother's Italian, so as a family, we [2]_____ (speak) two languages at home since I can remember. My parents [3]_____ (work) in six different countries, so I learned to speak English, Spanish and Arabic when I was at school. They're working in Singapore now. We [4]_____ (not live) in the same country for some years, but I visit them when I can. Moving around so much was hard at times, but it [5]_____ (help) me to adapt to the job I'm doing now – I [6]_____ (earn) my living as an interpreter for over a year, and I travel all the time. Do you have to travel for your work? And [7]_____ (you / ever / want) to live in another country?

I'll stop here as I'm really tired. My company [8]_____ (prepare) for an international conference, and I've got a busy day tomorrow.

Sasha

**Over to you**

How long have you been doing your current job or studies? Have you been busy recently? If so, what have you been doing?

**4** Complete the questions in this questionnaire about transferable skills using the words in the box. You do not need to use three of the words.

> balance   communicator   compromise   delegate   endurance   eyesight
> ~~fit~~   focused   imagination   listener   logically   manage   numbers
> reflexes   self-disciplined   sensitive   strong   well-organised

# Check out your transferable skills

Answer these questions to find out what skills you could bring to a new job.

**A Physical skills**

1  Are you physically ____fit____ ? Do you do sport or exercise regularly?     Yes / No
2  Do you have plenty of _____ ? Can you keep going and not get tired?     Yes / No
3  How good are your reactions? Have you got quick _____ ?     Yes / No
4  Are you steady on your feet? Have you got a good sense of _____ ?     Yes / No
5  What about your ability to see things? Have you got good _____ ?     Yes / No

**B Mental skills**

6  What was your maths like at school? Are you good with _____ ?     Yes / No
7  Are you good at solving problems? Are you able to think _____ ?     Yes / No
8  Can you avoid distractions when you're working? Are you _____ ?     Yes / No
9  Do you arrange and plan things carefully? Are you _____ ?     Yes / No
10  Do you work hard when the boss isn't there? Are you _____ ?     Yes / No

**C People skills**

11  Can you express your ideas well? Are you an effective _____ ?     Yes / No
12  Are you flexible when you're negotiating? Can you _____ ?     Yes / No
13  Do you give part of your work to others? Are you able to _____ ?     Yes / No
14  Can you control and organise others? Are you able to _____ groups?     Yes / No
15  Do you consider how other people feel? Are you _____ to their feelings?     Yes / No

## Over to you

Write similar questions for the three extra words in Exercise 4. Then answer all the questions. According to the questionnaire, do you have more physical, mental or people skills?

**5** Match the sentence halves to make some advice related to music.

| | |
|---|---|
| 1  Having some singing lessons ... | a  it helps. |
| 2  You don't need to read music, ... | b  can find places to play. |
| 3  If you can get other people to read your lyrics, ... | c  is to play at folk clubs. |
| | d  can help you. |
| 4  Listen to your playing. It helps ... | e  to record yourself. |
| 5  There are good things to be learned ... | f  if you can get some regular work. |
| 6  There are a number of ways you ... | g  but it helps. |
| 7  Leave a CD at bars or cafés and see ... | h  find a good manager. |
| 8  A good way of building up experience ... | i  from the biographies of |
| 9  If you really want to turn professional, ... |    successful artists. |

**6** Who is the advice in Exercise 5 for?

# EXPLOREWriting

**7** Look at the job advert. What skills and qualifications do you think it requires? Make a list.

**8** Read the covering letter below. Does the applicant mention any of the skills on your list?

> Mystic Comics are looking for a salesperson to join their international marketing team. Do you have the necessary qualifications, skills and experience? Send a CV and covering letter to applications@mysticcomics.com.

---

| Send | Save Now | Discard |
|------|----------|---------|

**B** *I* <u>U</u> 𝓕· T⊤· T▣ T⌀ ▣ ⊶ ⅛ ☰ ⫤ ⫥ 66 ☰ ☰ ☰ 𝐓ₓ &laquo; Plain Text     <u>Check Spelling</u> ▼

Dear Sir or Madam

I'm writing in response to you're advert for a salesperson at JobsOnlineNow.com. My ambition has always been to work in the comic publishing sector and I attach a copy of my CV for your consideration.

As you will see, I have ample sales experience and a degree in Marketing. Mystic Comics has a reputation around the world for the quality of its publications, and as a keen reader of your products, I would bring enthusiasm and knowledge to the job of selling them.

My previous sales experience has allowed me ot develop the skills that this position requires. I'm a good communicator, with the ability to listen to others and compromise. Self-discipline is another key skill in this field, and my positive sales record demonstrates my ability to remain focused when working alone. I am also able to make the most of difficult circumstances. I've been unemployed since my last company closed, but have been using my time to study Chinese. I'm sure this would be useful when dealing with international clients.

Thank you in advance fro considering my application. I can be available for an interview at any time, and look forward to hearing form you in the near future.

Yours faithfully

Susan James

---

**9** A covering letter or email is the first thing an employer reads, so it's vital to give the right impression. Look at the checklist below. Then read the covering letter in Exercise 8 again and tick the things it does.

**Your covering letter checklist** ☑
a It's addressed to a person in the company. ☐
b It says where I saw the advert. ☐
c It says why I'm interested in this job. ☐
d It shows I've researched the employer. ☐
e It matches my skills and experience to the employer's needs. ☐
f It says when I'm free for an interview. ☐
g The style is formal. ☐
h I haven't used contractions. ☐
i Spelling is correct throughout. ☐

**10** Find and correct four spelling mistakes and four contractions in the covering letter in Exercise 8.

**11** Choose one of the jobs below, or one you would like to do, and write a covering letter. <u>Underline</u> expressions in the letter in Exercise 8 that you could use.

| UK English | US English |
|------------|------------|
| CV | résumé |
| covering letter | cover letter |

an aerobics instructor    the office manager for a large company    a civil engineer
an advertising executive    a computer programmer    a video game designer

# Interview Hidden talents

**1** Before you watch, think about these questions.

Do you have a particular skill? How did you learn it? Do you use it in your professional life?

**2** Watch Clare and Carlos. What skill or talent do each of them talk about? Do they use it professionally? Circle Yes or No.

Clare's skill: _____ Yes / No

Carlos' skill: _____ Yes / No

Clare          Carlos

**3** Watch Clare again (0:11–1:03) and answer the questions. Use the glossary to help you.

1  When did she start learning her skill? _____

2  What does she do to develop her skill? _____

3  Name the four types of cake that she makes. _____

4  What has been her most difficult cake? Why? _____

**4** Complete these extracts from what Clare says. Write one word in each gap. Use the definitions in brackets to help you, and watch again if necessary.

1  It's something that I _____ _____ about three years ago now. (started doing)

2  I _____ _____ make money from making birthday cakes. (these words add emphasis)

3  I think the most difficult cake I've done _____ _____ is probably ... (until now)

4  I've done cakes for hen parties and _____ _____ , really. (a lot of different types)

5  That _____ _____ quite a lot of my time. (occupies)

**5** Watch Carlos again (1:06–3:04). Are the sentences true or false? Correct the false ones.

1  He has a clear memory of when he started writing.                                    TRUE / FALSE
2  Before he studied writing at school, he already had his own voice.                    TRUE / FALSE
3  His novel is a love story.                                                            TRUE / FALSE
4  He says that the characters developed as the story progressed.                        TRUE / FALSE
5  The story is told from the point of view of one character.                            TRUE / FALSE
6  His dream to publish a novel came true as a result of sending his novel to a publisher.  TRUE / FALSE

**6** Make as many collocations as you can with one word or expression from each box. Which ones does Carlos use? Watch again to check.

apply to   express   study   improve   publish          a novel   skills   yourself   a school   techniques

_____

_____

_____

_____

**7** Which skill would you most like to have, Clare's or Carlos'? Why? Is there a particular skill you would like to learn?

## GLOSSARY

**christening** (noun): a Christian ceremony at which a baby is given a name
**hen party** (noun): a party for women only, held for a woman before she is married
**tier** (noun): one of several layers or levels
**icing** (noun): a sweet food used to cover or fill cakes, made from sugar and water or sugar and butter

# Misunderstandings

**VOCABULARY**

Dealing with misunderstandings

**1** Put the words in the correct order to make phrases and sentences. Then match them with the gaps in the conversation below.

a meant / I / she / think  _I think she meant_ _____

b I / her / nearly finished it / I'd / told _____

c it / explains / that _____

d that report / you'd / I / thought / done _____

e to / is / another / text everyone / option _____

f thing / is / print it out / logical / to / the _____

g told / sent / us all a copy / you'd / she / me _____

h send / what / now / I / it / if _____

i she / not / said / what / that's _____

OPRAH     ¹ _d_ .

NOVAK     I have done it. Why do you ask?

OPRAH     Because I asked Sanya about it on Friday and ² ___ .

NOVAK     ³ ___ . But she said you didn't need it until today.

OPRAH     ⁴ ___ we needed it first thing today.

NOVAK     ⁵ ___ . She said *on* Monday.

OPRAH     Well, ⁶ ___ . The problem is, we're seeing a customer at ten and we need to discuss the report.

NOVAK     ⁷ ___ by email?

OPRAH     Not everyone's going to be at their desks, and we've only got half an hour to read it. ⁸ ___ and take a copy to everyone.

NOVAK     But how will I find them if they're not at their desks?

OPRAH     Good point. ⁹ ___ . Say there are copies in the conference room.

NOVAK     That sounds like the best idea.

**GRAMMAR**

Past simple and past perfect simple

**2** Write complete sentences using the prompts. Use one past simple and one past perfect form.

1 Why wasn't Lars at the barbecue on Sunday? I / think / you / invite / him.
    *I thought you had invited him.*

2 It / already / finish / when / he / hear / about it. _____

3 He / not read / my email _____ till Sunday night because / he / be away / for a few days. _____

4 The Lees didn't buy our car in the end. By the time / they / contact / us / we / sell / it. _____

5 We / assume / they / decide / not to buy it. _____

6 I was really late this morning. When I / get / to the station my train / already / leave. _____

7 I got on the next train. Then I / realise / I / take / the wrong one.
_____

8 The strange thing is, nobody / notice / that I / not arrive / on time.
_____

**3** Complete this travel story using the past simple or past perfect form of the verbs in brackets.

This happened last summer. We were travelling to Berlin to visit family and stopped for the second night in a hotel in Strasbourg. We ¹_____ (be) on the road for 10 hours at that point and we were very tired. I ²_____ (reserve) a room online, so we all ³_____ (get out) of the car with our luggage. There was a queue at reception, and when it was our turn, I ⁴_____ (hand) the receptionist the reservation that I ⁵_____ (print out). She shook her head and pointed at the children. There were four of us and we ⁶_____ (not book) a room for four. I ⁷_____ (explain) that both children were under five and that we ⁸_____ (sleep) in a room for three at one of their hotels the night before, but it was no use. So I asked for a room for four, but she ⁹_____ (tell) me the person before us in the queue ¹⁰_____ (take) the last one. We looked for another hotel in the area but they were all full, so in the end we decided to keep going, taking turns to sleep while the other drove through the night.

VOCABULARY

Adverbs for describing actions

**4** Complete the adverbs and/or their opposites.

1   carefully / care_____
2   suddenly / grad_____
3   reluct_____ / enthusiastic_____
4   deli_____ / accident_____
5   calm_____ / furi_____

**5** Complete this description of an incident at a dinner party using the adverbs from Exercise 4. Use each adverb once.

After moving into our new flat, we decided we should celebrate in some way. I love entertaining, so I ¹_____ suggested a dinner party. Henk didn't like the idea, but after some persuasion, he ²_____ agreed. We didn't want any problems, so ³_____ we selected a group of people to invite. However, we ⁴_____ forgot to find out about their eating habits. On the night, everything was going well until ⁵_____ Wilhelmina stopped eating. People ⁶_____ stopped talking and looked at her. 'I can see you ⁷_____ made some vegetarian options,' she said, 'but I think you've ⁸_____ put some meat in these lentils.' Others might have reacted ⁹_____, but Wilhelmina expressed herself ¹⁰_____ and politely. I immediately apologised, but Wilhelmina said there was no need. We continued eating in silence for a while, but people started talking again and eventually the incident was forgotten.

**6** Rewrite these sentences with the adverb in two different positions.

1   I enthusiastically suggested a dinner party.

_____
_____

2   Carefully we selected a group of people to invite.

_____
_____

3   People started talking again eventually.

_____
_____

**Over to you**

When did you last do something in these ways – enthusiastically, reluctantly, furiously, accidentally, carefully? Write sentences to describe the situations.

Past progressive
and past perfect
progressive

**7** Complete this version of a Greek story by Aesop using the past progressive or past perfect progressive form of the verbs in brackets.

One evening a woodsman [1]_____ (return) home. He [2]_____ (cut down) trees all day, and was tired, so he stopped to rest beside a lake. While he [3]_____ (rest), his axe fell into the water. Without his axe he couldn't work and feed his family, so the woodsman called to Zeus, the king of the gods, to help him. At first, Zeus ignored him, but he eventually lost patience. The woodsman [4]_____ (call) for help for several hours by now, so Zeus told the god Hermes to find the woodsman's axe and return it. 'But show him a golden axe too, and if he greedily takes that, cut off his head!' When Hermes arrived, the woodsman [5]_____ (still / sit) by the lake. Hermes put the two axes on the ground in front of him and asked him to choose one. He immediately chose his own. The golden axe that Hermes [6]_____ (carry) was very heavy, and he didn't want to take it back with him. So, as a reward for his honesty, Hermes gave the woodsman the golden axe too.

**8** Circle the correct verb form to complete these stories.

According to legend, the English folk hero Robin Hood [1]became / was becoming an outlaw because he [2]was killing / had been killing the king's deer – a crime punishable by death. He hid in Sherwood Forest, and it was while he [3]was hiding / had been hiding there that he started robbing rich travellers and giving money to the poor.

Did you hear that news story about a Korean woman who [4]finally got / was finally getting her driving licence after 950 attempts? She [5]was trying / had been trying to pass the written test for over four years and [6]had taken / was taking it every day except weekends and holidays.

Famous around the world for the statues of his Terracotta Army, Qin Shi Huang, the first Chinese emperor, [7]created / was creating one country out of states that [8]were fighting / had been fighting for over two centuries. His statues were discovered in 1974 by workmen who [9]looked / were looking for a place to dig a well.

Explaining a
complaint

**9** Complete the email complaint to a flower shop using the words in the box.

ended up   go to the trouble of   had   I'd been   said they'd   still hadn't
that cost me   they'd already   they said   was told   would

I'm writing to complain about the service in your Boston shop. It has ruined my wedding anniversary. I ordered some flowers first thing yesterday morning. I [1]_____ they'd arrive later in the morning. They didn't, so I phoned the shop. They [2]_____ written down my address incorrectly, and promised the flowers [3]_____ be with me mid-afternoon. At 4 o'clock they [4]_____ arrived, so I phoned again. They were engaged. I eventually got through at 5. By that time [5]_____ phoning for an hour. This time I was informed that it was too late for any more deliveries. I explained that [6]_____ failed to deliver the flowers before that, but [7]_____ their driver [8]_____ gone home. So I had to [9]_____ picking them up myself. But that wasn't all. I couldn't find a parking space, so I [10]_____ parking on a double yellow line and got a ticket. [11]_____ £50. I think under the circumstances you should refund the price of the flowers.

# EXPLOREReading

**10** What possible problems could people have with the supply of gas to their home? Make a list.

**11** Read the email and answer the questions.

1 Is the problem in the story on your list from Exercise 10?
2 Was the problem easy to solve?
3 This story was popular on the Internet. Do you think it is true? If not, why not?

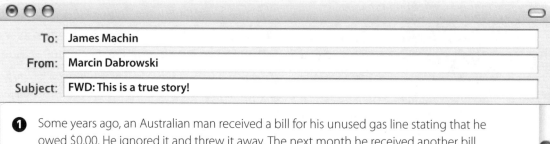

| | |
|---|---|
| To: | James Machin |
| From: | Marcin Dabrowski |
| Subject: | FWD: This is a true story! |

**1** Some years ago, an Australian man received a bill for his unused gas line stating that he owed $0.00. He ignored it and threw it away. The next month he received another bill and threw that one away too.

**2** The following month the gas company sent him a note stating they were going to cancel his gas line if he didn't send them $0.00 by return mail. He called them, and they said it was a computer error and they would take care of it.

**3** The month after that he decided to try out the gas line, figuring that if there was usage on the account it would put an end to this ridiculous predicament. However, when he went to use the gas, it had been cut off.

**4** He called the gas company, who apologised for the computer error once again and said that they would deal with it. The next day he got a bill for $0.00, stating that payment was now overdue. Assuming that the latest bill was yet another mistake, he ignored it, trusting that the company would sort the problem out.

**5** A month later he got a bill for $0.00. This bill also stated that he had 10 days to pay his account or the company would have to take steps to recover the debt.

**6** Finally, giving in, he thought he would beat the company at their own game and mailed them a cheque for $0.00. The computer processed his account and returned a statement to the effect that he now owed the gas company nothing.

**7** A week later, his bank manager called and asked him what he was doing writing a cheque for $0.00. After a lengthy explanation the bank manager replied that the $0.00 cheque had caused their cheque-processing software to fail. The bank could therefore not process ANY cheques they had received from ANY of their customers that day.

**8** The following month the man received a letter from the gas company claiming that his cheque had bounced and that he now owed them $0.00 and unless he sent a cheque by return mail they would take immediate steps to recover the debt.

**9** At this point, the man decided to file a debt harassment claim against the gas company. It took him nearly two hours to convince the clerks at the local courthouse that he was not joking. The matter was heard in the nearby Magistrates' Court and the gas company was ordered to pay the claimant's court costs and a total of $1,500 per month as compensation for the aggravation they had caused their client to suffer.

12 Put the events about the man in the story in order. Then read the story again to check.

a ___ He tried to use his gas line.

b ___ His bank didn't pay the money on the cheque.

c ___ The gas company turned off the gas to his house.

d ___ He took legal action against the gas company.

e ___ He sent a cheque to the gas company.

f ___ He received a first gas bill for $0.00.

g ___ His cheque made the bank's computers crash.

h ___ He first phoned the gas company.

13 Find four expressions in the story that mean the same as 'solve the problem'.

1 _____

2 _____

3 _____

4 _____

14 Find words in the story to complete these definitions.

1 A _____ is an unpleasant situation which is difficult to get out of. (Paragraph 3)

2 If a gas company cancels your line, they _____ your gas. (Paragraph 3)

3 If something is late, it is _____ . (Paragraph 4)

4 If you owe money, you are in _____ . (Paragraph 5)

5 A _____ is a printed record of the money put into and removed from an account. (Paragraph 6)

6 If a bank doesn't pay the money on a cheque, the cheque has _____ . (Paragraph 8)

7 If you take legal action against somebody in court, you _____ a _____ . (Paragraph 9)

8 Behaviour that is repeated and which annoys or threatens someone is _____ . (Paragraph 9)

**Over to you**

Have you ever had a problem like the one described in the story? If so, what was it? Was it easy or difficult to solve?

## GLOSSARY

**figure** (verb): to expect or think that something will happen
**usage** (noun): the amount of something that has been used
**beat somebody at their own game** (expression): to use to your own advantage the methods by which someone else has tried to defeat you
**aggravation** (noun): trouble or difficulty

**1** Before you watch, think about these questions.

Have you ever been on a holiday or trip that went wrong in some way? If so, tick (✓) any of these problems that you had.

| | | You | Emma |
|---|---|---|---|
| 1 | A flight was delayed | | |
| 2 | A car broke down | | |
| 3 | Some luggage got lost | | |
| 4 | There was terrible weather | | |
| 5 | Somebody was ill | | |
| 6 | The hotel was very noisy | | |

Emma

**2** Watch the video and tick (✓) the problems in Exercise 1 that Emma had on a childhood holiday.

**3** Watch Part 1 again (0:11–1:50). Find and correct five mistakes in this summary.

When Emma was seven years old she went on a caravan holiday with six other people. They set off in two cars, and an hour later one of the children was sick, so they had to stop to clean up. By the time they arrived at the caravan site, six people in the group had the sickness bug, and by the end of the holiday, everyone in the group had had it. While they were there, the people who were well slept in the caravan, and those who were ill slept in a house.

**4** Complete these extracts from what Emma says with the correct form of *one* verb. Then watch again to check.

1 It took us about seven hours in total to _____ down there.

2 The kids ... couldn't wait to _____ there.

3 Everyone had to pile out of the car, clean themselves up, _____ back in.

4 So everyone started to _____ a bit nervous and parents were kind of _____ a bit stressed out.

5 So the caravans _____ split into the sick caravan and the well caravan.

**5** Watch Part 2 again (1:53–3:25) and answer the questions.

1 How long was the holiday?

_____

2 Why were the children excited?

_____

3 Why did Emma's friend cover her face with a cushion?

_____

**6** Emma uses adjectives, comparisons and dynamic verbs to bring her story to life. Do you know what these words mean? How does she use them in her story?

1 steepest _____

2 banger _____

3 grabbed _____

4 petrified _____

5 smash into _____

6 leapt out _____

**7** Write a description of a real or invented holiday or trip on which things went wrong.

**GLOSSARY**

**sick** (adjective): ill, not well
**a bit of a hooha** (expression): a fuss; a disturbance that involves noisy complaints
**pile out** (verb): leave a place in large numbers, usually in a disorganised way
**bug** (noun): bacteria or a virus causing an illness that is usually not serious

# Learners and teachers

**VOCABULARY**

Discussing options

**1** Complete each group of three sentences using the words in brackets and other words so that they have a similar meaning to the first sentence.

**We're interested in the writing course.**

1  We _____*wouldn't mind doing*_____ the writing course. (mind / doing)

2  We _____ the writing course. (like / sound)

3  We'd _____ the writing course _____. (give / try)

**I need to choose between yoga and Tai Chi.**

4  I've _____ yoga and Tai Chi. (narrowed / down)

5  For me, _____ yoga _____ Tai Chi. (choice / or)

6  I'd _____ yoga or Tai Chi. (happy / either)

**She's not sure about flamenco classes.**

7  She _____ about flamenco classes. (make / mind)

8  She's _____ flamenco classes. (in / minds)

9  She's _____ flamenco classes. (mixed / feelings)

**I'm not interested in the chess club.**

10  The chess club _____. (really / thing)

11  _____ going to the chess club! (no / way)

12  The chess club _____. (appeal / me)

**VOCABULARY**

Work and commitment

**2** Complete each conversation about studying and training using the correct form of the verbs in the box and *on*, *out*, *towards* or *up*. Use each verb once.

carry   drop   give   keep   sign

A  I think I'm going to [1]_____ engineering. It's too much work.

B  But you knew that when you [2]_____ for the course. And you're doing well.

A  But I'm really busy. I'm also in the football team, in the theatre group ...

B  This is a full-time course. You can't expect to [3]_____ doing so many extra-curricular activities and [4]_____ your good grades. Why don't you choose one activity and focus on that? If you [5]_____ of university now, you'll leave with no qualification. I think you'll regret that in the future.

carry   sign   take   work (x2)

A  I wanted to see you about my job. I'm happy, but I've been here for five years, and I'd like to [6]_____ more responsibility.

B  That's good to hear, but to be considered for promotion you'll need to do more training. To start with, you'll need to [7]_____ your computer skills. You could [8]_____ for one of our lunchtime training programmes to achieve that. And in the longer term, you should perhaps [9]_____ getting an accountancy qualification. If you're interested, we could adapt your working hours so that you can [10]_____ working and study at the same time. Have a think about it and we can talk again.

3  Complete the crossword.

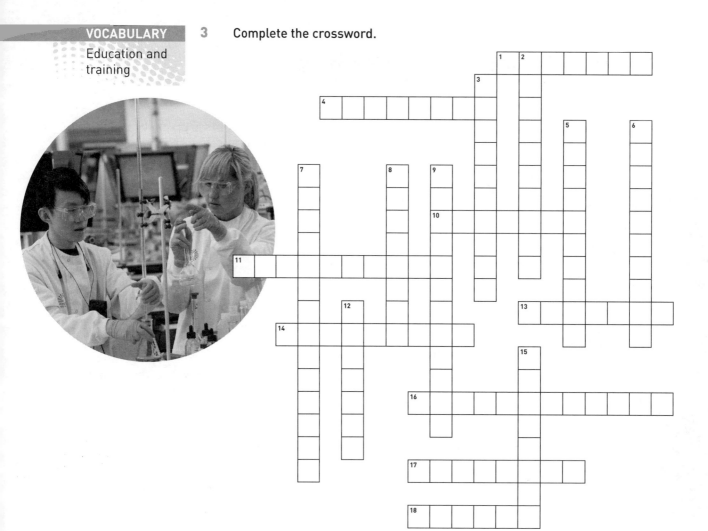

**Across**

1  _____ courses are for people who can't attend classes during the day. (7)

4  _____ learning consists of going to classes at a university. (2–6)

10  A _____ is an occasion when a teacher and a group of students meet to study and discuss something. (7)

11  _____ learning happens when teachers and students meet in the same place. (4-2-4)

13  In a _____ , a college or university teacher gives a formal talk on a specialist subject. (7)

14  At the end of many courses you have to take a _____ . (5, 4)

16  People who study at university at a more advanced level than a first degree do _____ courses. (12)

17  On a _____ course you spend the whole of the working week studying. (4-4)

18  _____ learning allows you to study where you want on the Internet. (6)

**Down**

2  _____ training provides skills and education that prepare you for a job. (10)

3  An _____ is a piece of work you give to your teacher as part of your studies. (10)

5  Work _____ is a period of time in which a student temporarily works for an employer. (10)

6  _____ is work set at regular periods as part of a course. (10)

7  On an _____ , you work for a skilled person for a period of time to learn that person's skills. (14)

8  On a _____ learning programme, you study at home by receiving and sending off work by post. (8)

9  A _____ is a long piece of writing on a particular subject that is done as part of a university course. (12)

12  _____ learning involves doing or using things rather than reading or learning about them. (5-2)

15  On _____ courses, you study for only some of the day or week. (4-4)

**Over to you**

Which of the education and training options in the crossword have you experienced? What were the benefits of each one?

Habits and
tendencies –
past and present

**4** Circle the correct options in this news article. If both are possible, circle them both.

# Are we too clean?

In some parts of the world, it seems that an obsession with cleanliness is causing a health problem. A parent's perception is often that children [1]are always getting / always used to get dirty. But the truth is that in countries like the UK, parents [2]clean / will clean their homes so thoroughly that children [3]hardly ever come / are hardly ever coming into contact with dirt, and therefore germs. The result is that one in three people today [4]will suffer / suffers from some kind of allergy – three times more than just ten years ago.

Parents who think back to how they [5]played / used to play as a child will see how much things have changed. Children today spend a lot of time in their rooms. Twenty years ago, our parents [6]thought / would think it was better for kids to play outside, so we [7]would probably spend / probably used to spend more time in the park than at home. We [8]would fall over and cut / were always falling over and cutting ourselves, but we [9]just brushed / would just brush ourselves clean and then kept on playing.

Now research seems to suggest that this was a good thing. An early contact with germs helps to protect our bodies against allergies later in life.

**5** Complete the questions using the verb forms in the box and the words in brackets. Use each verb form once.

> the past simple   *would*   *used to*   the present simple   *will*   *be always -ing*

1   Where _____ (your family / live) when you were a child?
2   _____ (the weather / be) different than it is now?
3   What games _____ (you and your friends / play) at school?
4   How often _____ (your family / eat) together these days?
5   What _____ (you / do) on a typical weekend?
6   _____ (you / send) text messages to your friends?

**Over to you**

Write your answers to the questions.

Describing a mentor

**6** Complete the words in these descriptions of mentors.

**1** An important influence in my life when I was young was my neighbour, Jamal. He [1]w_____ o_____ of those pe_____ w_____ isn't frightened of anybody. [2]He'_____ a_____ look people in the eye and say exactly what he thought. But he wasn't aggressive, and people respected him. [3]I'_____ n_____ known an_____ s_____ confident.

**2** My grandmother [4]w_____ a really po_____ in_____ o_____ me. She lived with us for some years, so we used to spend a lot of time together. She [5]w_____ t_____ most positive person I'_____ e_____ m_____. She had a hard life, but nothing was ever a problem, and she [6]w_____ n_____ get angry or depressed about things.

**3** My first tennis instructor [7]m_____ a very b_____ im_____ o_____ me. She [8]t_____ m_____ a lot a_____ self-discipline and how to control your emotions. If you let your emotions take over, you never do your best, and I think that's true in other areas of life, too. So I think I [9]o_____ her a lot.

# EXPLOREWriting

**7** Read the headlines and tick (✓) the ones that reflect an issue in your country. From your own experience, do you think the headlines you ticked are true?

**a** New technologies are responsible for poor reading and writing skills

**b** People today are unwilling to give up their seat to the elderly on public transport

**c** Pupils today have less respect for teachers, a new survey finds

**d** Children spending too much time at home, a report suggests

**e** MANY PARENTS' LIVES LESS HEALTHY THAN THEIR CHILDREN'S

**8** Read this letter, which was published in a newspaper. Which headline (a–e) in Exercise 7 does it comment on? Do you agree with the writer's point of view?

Your article was a <u>timely</u> reminder of <u>just how much</u> schools have changed, and it <u>rightly</u> linked a loss of respect for teachers to falling educational standards. However, it didn't look into the reasons behind this change, and I think there are lessons to be learned from the past.

Looking back at <u>my own school days</u>, we used to have <u>far more</u> respect for teachers. Obviously, some teachers would have more discipline problems than others. There were also teachers who were too strict, and we feared rather than respected them. But <u>in those days</u>, pupils <u>always</u> knew that disruptive behaviour would get them into serious trouble. And if our parents were called in to talk about a problem, they would <u>invariably</u> support the teacher.

<u>Nowadays</u>, it seems that parents are much more likely to defend their children, however bad their behaviour is, and will <u>constantly</u> blame the teacher for not being able to impose discipline. But if parents don't respect teachers, how can we expect their children to? Many changes are for the better, but <u>surely</u> we'd all benefit from a return to <u>the days when</u> teachers were respected.

**9** Which of these statements best summarises the writer's point of view?

a Things in the past were generally better than things today.
b With the exception of education, things today are better than they were in the past.
c Things often improve over time, but education is one of the exceptions.

**10** Which <u>underlined</u> expressions in Exercise 8 ...

1 tell you that something happens a lot? _____
2 emphasise a contrast? _____
3 refer to a period of time? _____
4 say that something is correct? _____
5 are used to persuade us that something is true? _____
6 indicate that it's a good moment for something to happen? _____

**11** Choose one of the other headlines and write a letter to a newspaper with your comments. Refer to your own experiences to support your point of view, and use expressions from Exercise 10 and any other useful expressions from the letter.

Carlos

Liu

**1** Before you watch, think about these questions.

Do you do, or have you ever done, any voluntary work? If so, what does/did it involve? Do/did you work with people?

**2** Watch the video. What voluntary work do Carlos and Liu do? What does their work have in common?

Carlos' work: _____

Liu's work: _____

They both: _____

**3** Who mentions these things? (Circle) *Carlos* or *Liu*. Match them with photos 1–4.

| | | | |
|---|---|---|---|
| pass | CARLOS / LIU | dribble | CARLOS / LIU |
| brush pen | CARLOS / LIU | ink drawings | CARLOS / LIU |

**❶**   **❷**   **❸**   **❹**

**4** Watch Carlos again (0:11–1:03) and complete these sentences about his work. Write one word in each gap.

1 He works with a football team in his local _____.

2 The team's called the _____ Colts.

3 His job is _____ work and what he does is a _____.

4 He feels he is _____ as a person as a result of his work.

**5** Watch Liu again (1:07–2:01) and answer the questions.

1 When and where did she start drawing?
2 Did her parents get angry? What did they do?
3 What did she study in Nottingham?

4 What did she do in Liverpool?
5 Where does she live now?
6 What did her students learn to write on Sunday?

**6** If you decided to teach something as part of a voluntary job, what would you teach? Would you prefer to work with adults or children? Why?

## GLOSSARY

**overwhelming** (adjective): very strong in effect or large in amount
**handcraft** (noun, Aus) / **handicraft** (noun, UK): a skilled activity in which something is made in a traditional way with the hands, or an object made by such an activity

# Local knowledge

**1** Rearrange the letters of the words in bold to complete these descriptions of local landmarks.

**1** The Headington Shark in Oxford, England, was created by sculptor John Buckley, and is a ¹_____ **calersiti**, life-sized model of a shark that sticks out of the roof of a house. A common first impression is that it was made to ²_____ **sumae** people, but its intention is more serious. The idea was to ³_____ _____ _____ **akem lopepe kinth** about the consequences of nuclear disasters like Chernobyl and Nagasaki and to ⁴_____ **ginfisy** a sense of impotence, anger and frustration.

**2** National Heroes Park in Kingston, Jamaica, contains a number of ⁵_____ **emmonnuts** that ⁶_____ **remacommeto** the most important people in Jamaica's history. Some are ⁷_____ **atnoditrail** in style and some, like the Monument in ⁸_____ **ohruno** of Samuel Sharpe pictured here, are more ⁹_____ **bractast**.

**3** David Govedare's ¹⁰_____ **dormen** ¹¹_____ **pluscuter** *The Joy of Running Together* is located in Spokane, Washington, in the USA and consists of ¹²_____ **utastes** of runners of all kinds. It ¹³_____ **braceslete** the tradition of Bloomsday, a large road race that is held every May.

**2** Complete the history of the Headington Shark using these words and expressions. There are two words and expressions you do not need to use.

> a big impression   a landmark   a lot of controversy   a tourist attraction
> an eyesore   erected   heavily criticised   opened to the public
> the urban landscape   to love it   to make of it   unveiled

The Headington Shark was ¹_____ on the roof of an ordinary home in Oxford on the 41st anniversary of the dropping of the atomic bomb on Nagasaki in Japan. It was done at night, with no warning or ceremony, and made ²_____ on local people when they saw it the following morning. It also attracted interest from media around the world, and for a while became ³_____. At first people didn't know what ⁴_____, and because of its size and location it caused ⁵_____. While some local people approved of it, it was ⁶_____ by other residents, who regarded it as ⁷_____. The local authorities wanted it taken down, claiming it was unsafe, but it was eventually allowed to stay. Many people who were negative about the shark grew ⁸_____ over time. It is still considered ⁹_____ in the city, but local people just see it as part of ¹⁰_____ now.

**3** Complete these descriptions from Exercise 2 in a different way, using the words and phrases in the box and adding other words as necessary.

| badly received by | baffled by | put up | warmed |
|---|---|---|---|

1 The Headington Shark _____ on the roof of an ordinary home.
2 While some local people approved of it, it _____ other residents.
3 At first people _____ it.
4 Many people who were negative about the shark _____ it over time.

---

**VOCABULARY**

Talking about well-known people

**4** Put the words in the correct order to complete these facts about two well-known people. Can you identify them?

Born in 1942 in Seattle, in the USA, [1]the / he / most / probably / famous / was _____ electric guitarist of the twentieth century.
After playing in a number of groups in the USA, [2]breakthrough / had / he / first / his _____ with some TV appearances in the UK.
[3]out / first / his / single / came _____ in 1966, and he released an album called *Are You Experienced* in 1967.
He was famous for his live performances. [4]his / one / of / was / techniques _____ to play the guitar with his mouth.
**Who was he?** _____

Born in Torquay in England in 1890, she is the best-selling writer of books of all time, although [5]as / nurse / she / a / out / started _____ .
Three of her poems were published in 1919, but [6]first / she / real / had / success / her _____ with the novel *The Mysterious Affair at Styles*.
[7]famous / of / is / most / works / her / one _____ *Murder on the Orient Express*, which was made into a successful film in 1974.
In 1955, [8]Grand Masters / won / for / a / Award / she _____ her work, a prize presented by the Mystery Writers of America.
**Who was she?** _____

---

**GRAMMAR**

Using the passive

**5** Complete the profile of Cuban singer Celia Cruz using the correct active or passive form of the verbs in brackets.

Celia Cruz was probably the most famous female singer in the history of Cuban music. Born in Havana in 1925, she [1]_____ (make) twenty-three best-selling albums and she [2]_____ (know) as the Queen of Salsa. When she was a teenager, she [3]_____ (took) to cabarets to sing, but her father [4]_____ (encourage) her to keep studying, hoping she would become a Spanish teacher. Her first major breakthrough [5]_____ (came) in 1950 when she [6]_____ (invite) to become the singer with a well-known orchestra, but she [7]_____ (not receive) well by audiences at first. In 1959, she [8]_____ (leave) Cuba and became a US citizen. From here, she travelled all over the world to give concerts. She [9]_____ (give) a first Grammy for her work in 1990. She died in 2003, but she [10]_____ (not forget). In 2004 a park in New Jersey [11]_____ (name) after her, and a star in her honour can [12]_____ (see) on a nearby sidewalk.

**Over to you**

Write about a famous person from where you live. Use some expressions from Exercises 4, 5 and 6.

**6** Complete the sentences about American writer J.D. Salinger using a passive form of the verb in bold in the first sentence.

1 We **know** very little about the writer J.D. Salinger, who died in 2010.

Very little _____ about the writer J.D. Salinger, who died in 2010.

2 People **say** that he became reclusive because he didn't like being famous.

It _____ that he became reclusive because he didn't like being famous.

3 You **can find** very few photos of him on the Internet.

Very few photos of him _____ on the Internet.

4 A publisher **published** his most famous book, *The Catcher in the Rye*, in 1951.

His most famous book, *The Catcher in the Rye*, _____ in 1951.

5 People **estimate** that 250,000 copies of the book are sold every year.

_____ that 250,000 copies of the book are sold every year.

6 Many teenagers still **read** the book as part of their school syllabus.

The book _____ by many teenagers as part of their school syllabus.

7 Publishers **have published** two biographies of the writer to date.

Two biographies of the writer _____ to date.

### VOCABULARY
Recalling details

**7** Complete the expressions in this conversation about Angkor Wat in Cambodia.

A So, when you were in Cambodia, did you see Angkor Wat?

B Of course! [1]I th_____ I'm ri_____ in sa_____ that it's the country's most visited tourist attraction.

A I'd love to see it. [2]I've h_____ t_____ it's one of the world's most amazing buildings.

B Yes, it's incredible. And it's really well preserved. [3]T_____ s_____ it was abandoned for many years, and that the huge moat around it protected it from being eaten up by the jungle.

A Do you know how old it is?

B [4]If I re_____ ri_____, it was built in the 12th century, so that's more than 800 years ago.

A And is it a temple?

B Yes, it is. I [5]r_____ so_____ that 'wat' means temple in Cambodian. As [6]f_____ a_____ I can re_____ it started out as a Hindu temple, and didn't become Buddhist until later.

### VOCABULARY
Describing a special occasion

**8** Match the sentence halves to make a description of the 'falles' festival in Valencia, Spain.

1 Traditionally, ...
2 In the old days, ...
3 Nowadays, ...
4 Thousands of people will ...
5 There can be anywhere ...
6 The festivities ...
7 There's ...
8 There will also ...
9 The reason they celebrate in Mar de Plata ...
10 On the 18th March, it's quite normal ...

a turn out to see the burning of the figures.
b to stay up all night dancing in the street.
c it's a festival to mark the arrival of spring.
d between seven and eight hundred figures.
e people burn the figures of politicians and other celebrities.
f a lot of music and fireworks.
g is because a lot of Valencian emigrants live there.
h people used to burn their old furniture on bonfires.
i be celebrations in other Valencian towns, and in Mar de Plata in Argentina.
j go on for five days.

# EXPLOREReading

9  How much do you know about Machu Picchu? Answer these questions.

1  Where is it? _____

2  Who was it built by? _____

3  How old is it? _____

4  When did Machu Picchu become known to the rest of the world? _____

5  Who told the rest of the world about it? _____

10  Read the website information about Machu Picchu and check or answer the questions in Exercise 9. Which question is not answered on the website?

# MACHU PICCHU ...
## LOST CITY OF THE INCAS

It's remarkable that Machu Picchu was first brought to the attention of the world in 1911. The Spanish invaders at the time of the Conquest and during centuries of colonial rule never discovered the city, and nobody ever led them there, suggesting that the site had long since been abandoned and forgotten. In fact, the outside world simply stumbled upon Machu Picchu, for it had never been lost to those who lived around it. Those same people eventually led the Hawaiian-born American explorer, Hiram Bingham, to the site in 1911.

Leaving Lima, the Peruvian capital, in July that year, Bingham travelled to Cusco to seek the last two capitals of the Inca, Vilcabamba and Vitcos. From Cusco, Bingham and his party journeyed on foot and by mule through the Urubamba Valley and into the Urubamba gorge. On July 23, they camped by the river at a place called Mandor Pampa, where they aroused the curiosity of Melchor Arteaga, a local farmer. Through his interpreter, Bingham learned that there were extensive ruins on top of the ridge opposite the camp, which Arteaga, in his native Quechua, called Machu Picchu, or 'old mountain'.

Accompanied by Arteaga and his interpreter, Bingham left the camp the following morning and reached the ridge at around midday. Here Bingham rested at a small hut where they enjoyed the hospitality of a group of peasant farmers. They told him that they had been living there for about four years and explained that they had found an extensive system of terraces on which they had decided to grow their crops. Bingham was then told that the ruins he sought were close by and was given a guide to lead him there.

Almost immediately, he was greeted by the sight of a broad sweep of ancient terraces that had recently been cleared of forest and reactivated. Led by the guide, he re-entered the forest beyond the terraces. Here his guide began to reveal a series of white granite walls which the historian immediately judged to be the finest examples of masonry that he had ever seen. They were, in fact, the remains of what we call today the Royal Tomb, the Main Temple, and the Temple of the Three Windows.

Other people had also seen, and even lived, at Machu Picchu, and had grown crops on the fertile soil that the Incas had carried up from the river valley to build Machu Picchu's magnificent 300-metre-high series of terraces, but these people had had neither the means nor the opportunity to bring the 'lost city' to the attention of the outside world.

**11** Read the information again and decide if the sentences are true or false. If false, explain why.

1   The Incas abandoned Machu Picchu before the Spanish invaded Peru.

_____

2   For a long time, local people didn't know that Machu Picchu existed.

_____

3   Bingham found Machu Picchu when he was travelling in the Urubamba gorge.

_____

4   Bingham found out that there were people living at Machu Picchu.

_____

5   Part of Machu Picchu was still covered in forest.

_____

6   People had only been growing crops at Machu Picchu for four years.

_____

**12** Find these words and phrases in the text about Machu Picchu.

1   A word meaning 'unusual and therefore surprising' (Paragraph 1)

_____

2   The name for the invasion of Peru by the Spanish (Paragraph 1)

_____

3   A period when a country is controlled by a more powerful and often distant country (Paragraph 1)

_____

4   A phrase meaning 'discovered by chance' (Paragraph 1)

_____

5   The name of a local language (Paragraph 2)

_____

6   The broken parts that are left from old buildings (Paragraph 3)

_____

7   A very hard rock used for building (Paragraph 4)

_____

8   The skill of building with stone (Paragraph 4)

_____

**13** Answer these questions in your own words.

1   Why is it 'remarkable' that the world didn't find out about Machu Picchu until 1911?
2   What is the writer saying in the final paragraph of the information?

## GLOSSARY

**ridge** (noun): a high edge along a mountain
**broad** (adjective): very wide
**sweep** (noun): a long, often curved, area of land

Rezarta

Liu

**1** Before you watch, think about these questions.

Have you ever shown someone from another country around your hometown? If so, what did you show them? What activities did you do? If not, what would you do with a foreign visitor in your hometown?

**2** Watch the video. What countries do Rezarta and Liu come from? What place names in their countries do they mention?

Rezarta: _____

Liu: _____

**3** Answer these questions about Rezarta and Liu's countries. Circle R, L, or *BOTH*. Then watch again to check.

Who ...
| | | |
|---|---|---|
| 1 | is going there in the near future? | R / L / BOTH |
| 2 | says that very few people in England know where it is? | R / L / BOTH |
| 3 | talks about changes there? | R / L / BOTH |
| 4 | mentions going there with her children? | R / L / BOTH |
| 5 | mentions at least one activity to do there? | R / L / BOTH |
| 6 | recommends that people visit it? | R / L / BOTH |
| 7 | talks about food? | R / L / BOTH |
| 8 | says what people there are like? | R / L / BOTH |

**4** Try to complete the missing word in these extracts from what Rezarta says. Watch again (0:11–1:20) to check.

1 Albania is sort of totally un_____ to a lot of people.

2 The country's un_____ (a) huge amount of change.

3 Even my children p_____ out various changes.

4 I would definitely en_____ everyone to go.

5 You might be pl_____ surprised – it's a fantastic country.

6 I think it will be quite an ex_____ for anyone.

**5** Watch Liu again (1:25–2:11). Are the sentences true or false? Correct the false ones.

| | | |
|---|---|---|
| 1 | Liu and her boyfriend will fly to China together. | TRUE / FALSE |
| 2 | Her boyfriend has been to China before. | TRUE / FALSE |
| 3 | They're going to cycle round the old city of Beijing. | TRUE / FALSE |
| 4 | Liu's parents live in Beijing. | TRUE / FALSE |
| 5 | Her parents are going to prepare Christmas dinner. | TRUE / FALSE |

**6** At the end of the video, Liu says about Christmas dinner that 'we don't have turkey' and that her parents are 'gonna make a chicken dinner, hopefully that'll do'. What do you think *do* means in this context?

a be possible     b be acceptable     c taste good

**7** Imagine some friends from another country are going to visit your country for two weeks. Recommend some places to see, and what the people should do there.

## GLOSSARY

**infrastructure** (noun): the basic systems, such as communication and transport, that a country or organisation uses in order to work effectively

**1** Complete the description of a famous painting by Pablo Picasso using the correct form of the verbs in the box.

> highlight   imply   portray   seem

Exhibited for the first time in 1937, Pablo Picasso's *Guernica* [1]_____ a scene from the bombing of the small Basque town of Guernica during the Spanish Civil War. The scene [2]_____ to take place in a room in which a mother is crying for the loss of her son. The tongues of the horse, the bull and the crying woman have been replaced by knives. This probably [3]_____ they are screaming, and the picture as a whole [4]_____ the powerlessness of the innocent victims who were caught in the attack.

**2** Find verbs in the description which you could replace with these verbs.

1 appears _____          3 suggests _____
2 emphasises _____        4 shows _____

**3** Complete the words in this conversation about a painting.

| | |
|---|---|
| JEN-CHEN | I think I've found a painting for the office. I'm sending you a photo of it now. |
| PABLO | I don't know. I [1]c_____ s_____ it in the office. I mean, it's the wrong [2]sh_____. It looks really wide. |
| JEN-CHEN | It's only 60 cm wide. |
| PABLO | OK, that's a good [3]s_____, but I'm not sure about the [4]st_____. You know I'm not keen on abstract art. |
| JEN-CHEN | But I really like the [5]c_____. All those reds and oranges. It's [6]n_____ and bright, and the office is really dark. It'd [7]m_____ it f_____ lighter. |
| PABLO | I think it [8]wo_____ l_____ nicer in the kitchen. It [9]co_____ g_____ above the cooker. |
| JEN-CHEN | It's obvious you don't like it, but I do. Maybe the office isn't the right place, but I [10]c_____ im_____ it in the living room, behind the sofa. |
| PABLO | But it [11]wo_____ s_____ our living room. It's too modern. |
| JEN-CHEN | I think it'd look good there, but let's try it first, and if we don't like it we [12]co_____ p_____ it in the bedroom. |
| PABLO | OK, let's try that. |

**VOCABULARY**
Discussing design

**4** Complete these words and expressions which have a similar meaning using the endings in the box. You will need to use some endings more than once.

-able  -ally  -el  -forward  -ful  -ic  -ing  -ive

1 low-key = unobtrus_ive_
2 green = environment_____ friendly
3 attract_____ = aesthet_____
4 long-last_____ = dur_____
5 nov_____ = innovat_____
6 honest = straight_____
7 meaning_____ = purpose_____

**5** Match the comments (a–g) about different products with the best pair of words and expressions (1–7) in Exercise 4.

a This car claims it's got lower carbon dioxide emissions than any other car on the market. ☐

b The batteries in this laptop are amazing. You can work for eight hours before they run out. ☐

c I love this camera. It's simple to use and does exactly what it says it does: take great pictures. ☐

d I never thought a fridge could be cool, but this one looks fantastic. ☐

e Look at this phone. It's a video camera, TV, credit card and front-door key too! Amazing. ☐

f This suitcase is really well designed. Even the smallest details have a function. ☐

g These speakers are great. They're small and have no cables, so you never notice them. ☐

**Over to you**

Write about some designs that you like using the adjectives and expressions in Exercise 4.

**GRAMMAR**
Describing objects – past participle clauses

**6** Cross out words to leave a description of the invention of the zip with six participle clauses.

The zip, which is known as a zipper in US English, is a fastening device that is used on clothes, bags and camping equipment. It was first patented in 1891, but it didn't become a practical alternative to buttons until years later. Early versions, which were made only of metal, used hooks and eyes, but they came apart easily. A zipper that was based on interlocking teeth was invented by the Swedish engineer Gideon Sundback in 1914, and this is the system that is used in zips around the world today.

Tim Berners-Lee

**7** **Add commas to these sentences about the World Wide Web where necessary.**

1   The World Wide Web used by millions of people around the globe is considered a design classic.
2   There is an early mention of the concept in a story written by Murray Leinster in 1946.
3   Developed in 1990 by Tim Berners-Lee the Web revolutionised our search for information.
4   Originally the Web was a system developed to help scientists share data.
5   The first-ever web browser called the World Wide Web couldn't show graphics in web pages.
6   Berners-Lee recently admitted that the // used in web addresses was a mistake.

**8** **Look at the descriptions of three products. Use participle clauses to write all the information in one sentence about each product. Delete words and use commas as necessary. Can you name the products?**

1   It was first launched in 1985. It's an operating system. It's installed on millions of computers.

_____

**Product:** _____

2   This object is a popular pen. It's called a *biro* in English. It was invented by a Hungarian newspaper editor.

_____

**Product:** _____

3   It was designed by Harry Beck in 1931. This map was a revolutionary concept. It's used today by transport systems around the world.

_____

**Product:** _____

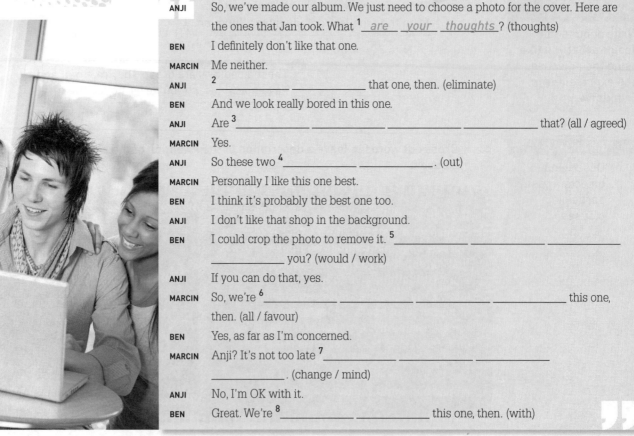

**9** **Three musicians are choosing a photo for their album cover. Complete the conversation with the words in brackets and one or two other words.**

ANJI   So, we've made our album. We just need to choose a photo for the cover. Here are the ones that Jan took. What [1] _are_ _your_ _thoughts_? (thoughts)

BEN   I definitely don't like that one.

MARCIN   Me neither.

ANJI   [2] _____ _____ that one, then. (eliminate)

BEN   And we look really bored in this one.

ANJI   Are [3] _____ _____ _____ _____ that? (all / agreed)

MARCIN   Yes.

ANJI   So these two [4] _____ _____. (out)

MARCIN   Personally I like this one best.

BEN   I think it's probably the best one too.

ANJI   I don't like that shop in the background.

BEN   I could crop the photo to remove it. [5] _____ _____ _____ _____ you? (would / work)

ANJI   If you can do that, yes.

MARCIN   So, we're [6] _____ _____ _____ _____ this one, then. (all / favour)

BEN   Yes, as far as I'm concerned.

MARCIN   Anji? It's not too late [7] _____ _____ _____ _____. (change / mind)

ANJI   No, I'm OK with it.

BEN   Great. We're [8] _____ _____ this one, then. (with)

# EXPLORE**Writing**

**10** Which do you think is the best innovation of the 21st century? Look at the website below and make your choice.

---

**Best innovation of the 21st century (so far!)**

Which is the most impressive innovation of the 21st century? Choose from the list below, or, if you think we've missed something, add your own choice in the box. Then write and tell us why you chose it!

○ High Definition TV  ○ Social networking sites (e.g. Facebook)
○ iPhone  ○ Wikipedia
○ iPod  ○ Twitter
○ Netbooks  ○ YouTube
○ WI-FI  ○ Skype

My choice(s): [                              ]

---

**11** Read this posting on the website. Which innovation has the writer chosen?

**posted at 11:23am**

There have been a lot of great innovations this century. For instance, there's Wikipedia, which has revolutionised the way we look for information. Then there are social networking sites such as Facebook, which have helped millions of people to keep in touch with friends – and make new ones.

But if I had to choose one, I'd go for _____. Not only is it one of the most useful gadgets I've ever owned, but it's also really aesthetic. It's very straightforward to use too, designed for people (like me) who are not really into technology. You don't need to read an instruction manual to make it work, because it's really intuitive. And it's got a touch screen, which means you can easily teach yourself to use it.

But what I really love about it is that for such a small gadget, it's absolutely packed with functions. For example, you can make calls, listen to music, take photos and connect to the Internet. I use mine to record music and even to tune my guitar. And all that in a pocket-sized piece of technology!

**12** Complete this extract from the posting, then read it again to check your answer.

Not only _____ one of the most useful gadgets I've ever owned, but it's also really aesthetic.

Now complete these sentences with **is**, **can** or **does**. Which innovations from the list in Exercise 10 do you think they refer to?

1 Not only _____ you watch lots of videos, but you can also upload your own videos. **Innovation:** _____

2 Not only _____ it free, but it also contains information about every topic imaginable. **Innovation:** _____

3 Not only _____ it allow you to make free phone calls, but it also allows you to do video conferencing. **Innovation:** _____

**13** Find and underline in the posting:

1 four words and phrases used to introduce examples.
2 three *which* clauses used to give extra information.
3 a non-defining past participle clause.

**14** Write a posting with your choice for the best innovation of the 21st century. Explain why you have chosen it. Use some of the language from Exercises 12 and 13 and other useful expressions from the posting.

# Before you watch

**1** What is the connection between the words in each of the groups?

| | | | | |
|---|---|---|---|---|
| 1 | lecturer | sculptor | social worker | student |
| 2 | drawing | sculpture | illustration | painting |
| 3 | metal | wire | rod | papier-mâché |
| 4 | to weld | to join | to stick together | to cut |
| 5 | bit | silhouette | shape | structure |

Which word is different in each group? Explain why. There may be more than one correct answer.

**2** Which words from Exercise 1 are illustrated in pictures 1–3 below?

_____     _____     _____

# While you watch

**3** In the video, Tony and Jayne talk about themselves and about working together. Watch the complete video. Who talks about (and doesn't simply mention) these things? Circle *T*, *J* or *BOTH*.

Tony          Jayne

1 Why I started sculpting    T / J / BOTH
2 The type of things I make    T / J / BOTH
3 How I met Jayne/Tony    T / J / BOTH
4 How I make a sculpture    T / J / BOTH
5 My ambition as an artist    T / J / BOTH

**4** Watch Part 1 again (0:09–2:24). Are the sentences about Tony true or false? Correct the false ones.

| | | |
|---|---|---|
| 1 | Tony comes from Cambridge originally. | TRUE / FALSE |
| 2 | He works at a university. | TRUE / FALSE |
| 3 | He only started producing art recently. | TRUE / FALSE |
| 4 | His first work in metal was a bicycle. | TRUE / FALSE |
| 5 | The bicycle didn't work very well. | TRUE / FALSE |
| 6 | He didn't want Jayne to come and watch him. | TRUE / FALSE |

**5** Watch again and complete the fact file about Jayne.

Name: _Jayne Ruffell-Ward_ _____     First profession: _____

Age: _____     How she got into sculpting: _____

Family: _____     _____

Studies: _____     _____

**6** Watch Part 2 again (2:27–3:04) and make notes about three steps that Tony takes when he starts a sculpture.

Step 1: _____ .

Step 2: _____ .

Step 3: _____ .

**7** Watch Part 3 again (3:08–5:06) and answer the questions.

1 Apart from specific technical skills, what has Jayne learned from Tony?
2 How did Tony work before he met Jayne?
3 What does he value about working with someone else?
4 What characteristics make Tony a fantastic teacher?
5 What view of art do they share?
6 What's the difference between them?
7 According to Jayne, what does Tony hope his art will do?
8 What three things is Jayne thankful to Tony for? Why?

**8** Watch Part 4 again (5:10–5:57) and complete the sentences.

1 At first, Tony says his favourite sculpture is _____ .

2 His ambition is _____ .

3 His favourite sculpture is of _____ .

4 The sculpture is about _____ .

# After you watch

**9** Complete these extracts from the video. Add the correct particles to the multi-word verbs.

1 Tony: Straight away I **got** _____ making animals and so on then I really haven't **looked** _____ .

2 Jayne: I came to Cambridge in the early nineties to study illustration and after that **ended** _____ doing social work, so, to **get** _____ _____ my art I was **looking** _____ _____ things.

3 Jayne: I wrote a letter saying, please could I come and you could show me how to **stick** pieces of metal _____ .

4 Jayne: He's taught me how to **break** the process _____ into manageable bite-sized pieces.

5 Jayne: That encouraging nature just **brings** _____ the best in people.

6 Tony: Well, I do actually and it **turns** _____ , it **turned** _____ after **putting** the two _____ , to be a little child whispering to his grandad.

**10** Would you like to work as an artist? Why? / Why not?

---

**GLOSSARY**

**lecturer** (noun): someone who teaches at a British college or university

**tandem** (noun): a bicycle made for two people who sit one behind the other

**social work** (noun): work that provides help and support for people who need it

**silhouette** (noun): a dark shape seen against a light surface

**stuff** (noun): an informal word used to refer to a substance or material

**rod** (noun): a long thin pole

**weld** (verb): to join two pieces of metal together permanently by melting the parts that touch

**plasma cutter** (noun): a tool that uses hot gas to cut things

**wire** (noun): a piece of thin metal thread which can be bent

**bite-sized** (adjective): describes something that is small enough to put in your mouth whole

**papier-mâché** (noun): pieces of paper mixed with glue or with flour and water and used to make decorative objects or models

**expertise** (noun): a high level of knowledge or skill

**springboard** (verb): to provide the opportunity to follow a particular plan of action, or the encouragement that is needed to make it successful

# 6 Virtual worlds

**1** Put these expressions in a logical chronological order, from 1 to 5.

___ be arrested        ___ go to prison        ___ be suspected

___ be sentenced      ___ be accused

**2** Complete these news stories with crime and justice words.

**a**

A York mother has been given a ¹_____ of £75 for feeding the ducks at her local park – but her daughter was allowed to carry on, as under English ²_____ she was too young to prosecute.

**b**

Twin brothers who were ³_____ for robbery in Berlin have been released. The twins are ⁴_____ of stealing £5.6m of jewellery and watches, but police can't prove which one was responsible.

**c**

A man from Poland has finally won an 18-month legal battle to clear his name. The man was ⁵_____ of kicking his neighbour's bucket.

**d**

The Dutch creator of a computer virus that infected computers around the world was ⁶_____ to 150 hours of ⁷_____ service on Thursday.

## Over to you

Write a short description of a crime that has been in the news recently.

**e**

A German bank manager who transferred millions of pounds from wealthy clients to customers in debt will not go to ⁸_____. The woman, called the 'Robin Hood Banker' by the press, was given a 22-month suspended ⁹_____.

**3** Decide which *two* of the expressions on the left in 1–4 can be used to make the relationship between the two sentences clearer. Then rewrite the sentences twice, using one of the possible expressions each time. You may need to join the sentences or add commas.

### Tips when choosing and using computer passwords_

| that way   or   then | 1  Include letters and numbers. Your password will be harder to guess. |
| --- | --- |

_____

_____

| otherwise   or else   that way | 2  Change your password regularly. Someone could see and remember it. |
| --- | --- |

_____

_____

| if not   then   that way | 3  Memorise and destroy your password. Nobody will find it. |
| --- | --- |

_____

_____

| or   then   if not | 4  It's important to sign out after every session. Others could access your information. |
| --- | --- |

_____

_____

## VOCABULARY
Reporting points of view

**4** Put the words in the correct order and add *one* extra word to complete these points of view about file sharing.

¹music companies / that / the  _The music companies say that_  file sharing is killing the music business. ²that / tell / they'll _____ album sales have fallen dramatically over recent years. ³concerned / as / they're / far _____ , people are simply stealing their products.

⁴also / there's / that / argument _____ in the end, it's the musicians who suffer the most.

⁵have / the / people / other / on / that / hand, / you / say _____ the Internet is starting a revolution. ⁶will / that / new groups / many _____ it's better for them to sell directly to their fans. ⁷they / that / say / what _____ they can sell their music more cheaply that way. ⁸people / think / lot of / that _____ music will survive without the music companies.

## GRAMMAR
Conditional clauses – present and future

**5** Which of the linking expressions below can you use to complete this forum posting about sharing films? Write all the possible letters (a–e) in the gaps.

a if
b as long as
c even if
d provided
e unless

**Posted on Mon 17 at 16.36:**

In my experience, most people will go to the cinema ¹___a___ they really want to see a new film, especially if the special effects are good. They'll also buy a home copy of a film they like ²_____ it's cheap enough. But people have very different attitudes to sharing films. Some people would never illegally download a film. Others wouldn't do it ³_____ buying a copy was really expensive. And then there are those who would share films ⁴_____ the cinema was free! That's because downloading films takes no time at all ⁵_____ you have a good internet connection, and for the moment at least, nothing happens to you if you do.

**6** Write real or unreal conditional sentences. Both options may be possible, depending on how you see the situation.

1 If someone / be caught / sharing files online, they / should lose / their internet connection.

_____

2 I / not watch / an illegal copy of a film even if a friend / give / it to me.

_____

3 People / pay / to read online newspapers as long as the cost / be / reasonable.

_____

4 I / not upgrade / my computer unless my current one / stop / working.

_____

5 I / do / all my banking on the Internet, provided it / be / completely safe.

_____

## Over to you
Which sentences do you agree with? Change any that you don't agree with to make them true for you.

**VOCABULARY**

Describing changes

**7** Match verbs 1–6 with verbs a–e. There is one extra verb you do not need to use.

| | | | |
|---|---|---|---|
| 1 | connect | a | cut |
| 2 | shift | b | link |
| 3 | drop | c | swap |
| 4 | leave | d | stick |
| 5 | place | e | move |
| 6 | switch | | |

**8** Gregori has asked Irene to look at his website. Complete Irene's reply with verbs from Exercise 7. If two verbs are possible, write them both.

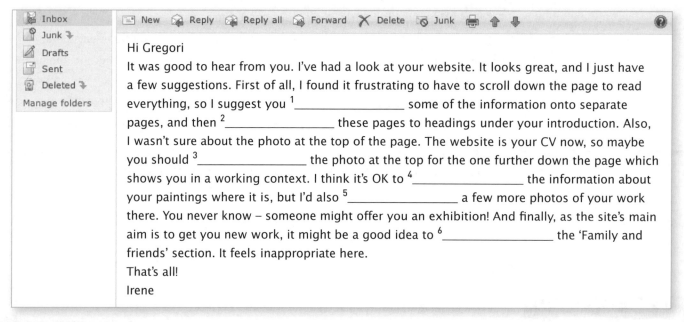

| Inbox | ✉ New  ↩ Reply  ↩ Reply all  ➡ Forward  ✗ Delete  🚫 Junk  🖨  ⬆  ⬇ | ? |
| Junk |
| Drafts |
| Sent |
| Deleted |
| Manage folders |

Hi Gregori

It was good to hear from you. I've had a look at your website. It looks great, and I just have a few suggestions. First of all, I found it frustrating to have to scroll down the page to read everything, so I suggest you ¹_____ some of the information onto separate pages, and then ²_____ these pages to headings under your introduction. Also, I wasn't sure about the photo at the top of the page. The website is your CV now, so maybe you should ³_____ the photo at the top for the one further down the page which shows you in a working context. I think it's OK to ⁴_____ the information about your paintings where it is, but I'd also ⁵_____ a few more photos of your work there. You never know – someone might offer you an exhibition! And finally, as the site's main aim is to get you new work, it might be a good idea to ⁶_____ the 'Family and friends' section. It feels inappropriate here.

That's all!

Irene

**VOCABULARY**

Habits and customs

**9** Complete the conversations using the words and expressions in the boxes.

I'd always   if   if it's (x2)   I'll definitely   I'll probably
there's no way I'd   wouldn't dream of

**A** Do you send people birthday cards?
**B** It depends who it is. ¹_____ a friend, then ²_____ send an email or an e-card, or maybe a text message. But ³_____ a family member, then ⁴_____ send a card. I mean, ⁵_____ it was my grandmother's birthday, I ⁶_____ sending her an email. She never checks her emails anyway.
**A** Right. ⁷_____ send my grandparents an email either. As for mates, ⁸_____ send a text message. It's quick and easy.

**Over to you**

What do you do for people's birthdays?

expected to   if you   increasingly common
really important   the proper thing to do   unheard of

**A** Can I ask your advice? We've been having problems with someone in the office, and I think we're going to have to fire him.
**B** Does he know? ⁹_____ are considering firing someone, it's ¹⁰_____ that you give them a formal warning first. It's ¹¹_____ for people to take companies to court for unfair dismissal.
**A** He knows. I've spoken to him on numerous occasions. The question is, how do you do it? Is writing a letter considered ¹²_____? It would be good if I could just email him.
**B** Don't even consider that. It's ¹³_____ to fire someone by email. You're ¹⁴_____ tell the person face to face, I think, *and* let them know why in writing.

# EXPLOREReading

**10** Answer the questions about computer hacking.

    1   What do you know about computer hacking?

    2   Do you regard it as a serious crime?

    3   Have you ever been a victim of computer hacking, or do you know of an organisation that has? If so, what was the result of the hacker's activity?

**11** Read the headline of the news article. What exactly do you think the article is going to be about? Make your prediction. Then read the article to find out if you were right.

## NEWSONLINE

### Looking to develop your IT career? Consider a course in ethical hacking.

**1** With computer crime on the rise, there's a growing need for security experts. But people in the IT world are often unable to take time off work to undergo the necessary training. That's where flexible courses in professional computer hacking or *ethical hacking* come in.

**2** An ethical hacker's job is to test computer networks against attacks by malicious hackers. Courses which teach the techniques used to carry out such tests are not new, but the way they are being delivered is. In addition to face-to-face classes, students are being offered the chance to study online at home or in the workplace, offline using self-study materials, or on the move with material they can download onto their mobile phones.

**3** Ethical hacking has grown as a professional field over the last few years as companies have become more aware of the threat that criminals pose to their computer networks. It's a threat that has also passed into public consciousness due to increased coverage in the media and cases of computer crime in TV series like *CSI* and *24*. Computer hackers can get into a computer system, steal data and erase their tracks in just 20 minutes, so IT professionals who decide to add ethical hacking to their CV are finding that their services are in constant demand.

**4** Training courses work on the principle that to stop a criminal, you need to learn to think like one. Students master the technologies that hackers use, such as denial-of-service attacks on computer systems. They also find out how to create computer viruses and about the social engineering techniques that hackers often use to trick people into divulging confidential information. Once in employment, their job consists of defending their client's computer network. This work will involve testing the network for security weaknesses by launching attacks in the form of dummy raids and penetration tests.

**5** The goal of training courses is to prepare students to take the online *Ethical Hacker* exam 312-50. This is organised by the Albuquerque-based International Council of Electronic Commerce Consultants, or EC-Council, the computer security industry's most widely recognised body. By passing the exam, students become a *Certified Ethical Hacker*, or 'white hat', as they are known in the field.

**6** However, as those who obtain the qualification acquire skills that could very easily be used for criminal gain, students have to sign an agreement stating that they will not use their new knowledge for illegal, 'black hat' hacker activities. They also need to demonstrate that they work for a legitimate company before they are accepted onto an EC-Council accredited course.

**12** **Read the article again and answer the questions in your own words.**

1 Why are flexible courses in ethical hacking popular with IT professionals?

_____

2 How many different ways can you study ethical hacking? Which ways are relatively new?

_____

3 What has helped to make the general public more aware of the dangers posed by hackers?

_____

4 What makes hackers such a dangerous threat?

_____

5 What similarities are there between an ethical hacker and a criminal one?

_____

6 What do students hope to get at the end of the course? Why is this important?

_____

7 Why do courses have to be careful about who they accept?

_____

8 What do all students on accredited courses have in common?

_____

**13** **Find these techniques in the article and match them with the definitions (1–4). Use the context to help you.**

a denial-of-service attack
b social engineering
c dummy raid
d penetration test

1 A method for evaluating a computer system's security. ☐
2 A simulated (= not real) attack on a computer system. ☐
3 Using manipulation in order to get people to give you private details. ☐
4 An attack that makes a computer system unavailable to the people who need to use it. ☐

**14** **Find preposition + noun phrases in the article to match to these definitions.**

1 increasing (Paragraph 1): _____
2 where you work (Paragraph 2): _____
3 when you are travelling (Paragraph 2): _____
4 with a lot of people needing your services (Paragraph 3): _____
5 with a job (Paragraph 4): _____
6 in a particular professional area (Paragraph 5): _____

**Over to you**

Would you like to study to be an ethical hacker? Why? / Why not?

Qusay

Ekapop

**1** **Before you watch, think about these questions.**

How important is the Internet to you in your daily life? Tick (✓) any sentences below that coincide with your opinion or experience of the Internet.

|   |   | **You** | **Qusay** | **Ekapop** |
|---|---|---|---|---|
| 1 | It allows me to see how people live in other parts of the world. |  |  |  |
| 2 | It's a good place to do your shopping. |  |  |  |
| 3 | It's changing some traditions in my country. |  |  |  |
| 4 | We'll all spend more time in virtual online worlds like Second Life in the future. |  |  |  |

**2** **Watch the video and tick (✓) the things in Exercise 1 that Qusay and Ekapop say about the Internet.**

**3** **What special thing do Qusay and Ekapop both talk about? What difference is there in the way that they talk about this thing?**

**4** **Watch Qusay again (0:11–1:02) and complete this summary of what he says. Write one word in each gap.**

The Internet has had a big [1]_____ in his country, and he sees it as a [2]_____ on other parts of the world. He says that as a result of the Internet, some traditional [3]_____ are changing. One example is [4]_____ ceremonies. Some brides will look on the Internet to find a special [5]_____ with a nice [6]_____ .

**5** **Watch Ekapop again (1:06–2:41) and answer the questions.**

1 Why did Ekapop go into Second Life?
2 How does he say people in Second Life get their character?
3 What does he say Second Life characters can do?
4 Why are companies taking more interest in Second Life now?
5 What *didn't* Ekapop do in Second Life?
6 Why does he think that other people do what he didn't do?

**6** **Match the two halves of these extracts from what Ekapop says. Watch again to check.**

| | | | |
|---|---|---|---|
| 1 | You don't actually ... | a | in spending a lot of money just to buy special clothes. |
| 2 | I've got to ... | b | want to spend that money. |
| 3 | I didn't see a huge benefit ... | c | own it at the end of the day. |
| 4 | I can see why people ... | d | make yourself, you know, stand out. |
| 5 | You might ... | e | know more of the technology. |

**7** **Do you take part in Second Life? If so, write an email trying to persuade a friend to take part too. If not, write an email to a friend who takes part explaining why you do or don't want to take part.**

---

## GLOSSARY

**Second Life** (noun): a virtual world which you can inhabit, and in which you can interact with others
**avatar** (noun): an image which represents you in online games, chatrooms, etc.

# 7 Inspiration

**1** (Circle) the correct words to complete these opinions.

## Streetview – your views on day-to-day issues

# What's the best way to deal with a problem?

Kayin, Nigeria

'I've always thought that the best way to [1]solve / come up with a problem is to [2]ignore it / work it out until you can't any more. You can [3]mull over / figure out a problem for days, thinking about this solution or that solution. But often, [4]giving up on / sorting out a problem only takes a few minutes, so all that thinking is a waste of energy. My advice is to [5]put off / tackle solving a problem until you really need to [6]come up with / find the answer to a solution. It's less stressful that way!'

Bo, China

'My personal technique for [7]finding the answer to / putting off a problem is to [8]concentrate on it / sort it out really hard for fifteen minutes. If in that time I can't [9]mull over / work out what to do, I [10]concentrate on it / give up on it for a while and do other things. Then, later in the day, I [11]solve it / tackle it again for fifteen minutes. I usually find that after two or three of these fifteen-minute sessions I've [12]figured out / ignored what to do.'

## Over to you

Which person is more similar to you – Kayin or Bo? Explain why, and point out any differences.

**2** Complete the expressions in this email from Lara to her aunt in Australia.

---

**Send**  **Save Now**  **Discard**

**B** *I* <u>U</u> *F* · T̄· T̄ₐ T̄ₒ 🖼 🔗 ⌸ ⌸ ⌸ ⌸ 66 ▤ ▤ ▤ T̄  « Plain Text                **Check Spelling** ▼

Dear Aunt Charlotte,

Thank you for your email. It was good to hear from you.

Since I last wrote I've had to find a new flat. This wasn't easy. [1]The b_____ pr_____ w_____ that rents have gone up a lot since I first came to live here, so [2]I f_____ i_____ really di_____ to find somewhere I could afford. Eventually, I found a small flat right at the top of an old six-storey building. [3]This pr_____ m_____ w_____ a real problem, as there was no way to get my piano up the stairs. In the end, [4]w_____ I d_____ to d_____ w_____ to sell it and buy myself a keyboard with the money. But as soon as I moved in, I realised I had another problem. The flat overlooks a square with lots of cafés in it, and it's noisy till late at night. After two weeks of sleepless nights I was desperate. [5]My w_____ o_____ so_____ this problem was to buy earplugs, and I've slept like a log ever since. So moving was stressful, but educational in its own way. [6]W_____ I l_____ w_____ that a problem sometimes depends on how you look at it. I obviously wasn't going to make the people in the square be quiet, so I was forced to find another way to deal with noise.

That's my news. How are things in Sydney?

Love, Lara

---

VOCABULARY
Inspiration

**3** Match the sentence halves and then use them to complete the descriptions below on a website for an artistic show. Write the sentence numbers in the gaps.

| | | | |
|---|---|---|---|
| 1 | My music is inspired ... | a | me at a concert |
| 2 | When I got my first PC I realised ... | b | using original music in the show from Nico |
| 3 | The idea for the show came to ... | c | by the sounds of the city |
| 4 | Even traffic noise can give you ... | d | that I could make music with that |
| 5 | I got the idea for ... | e | from things I see around me |
| 6 | I get my inspiration ... | f | the idea for a piece of music |

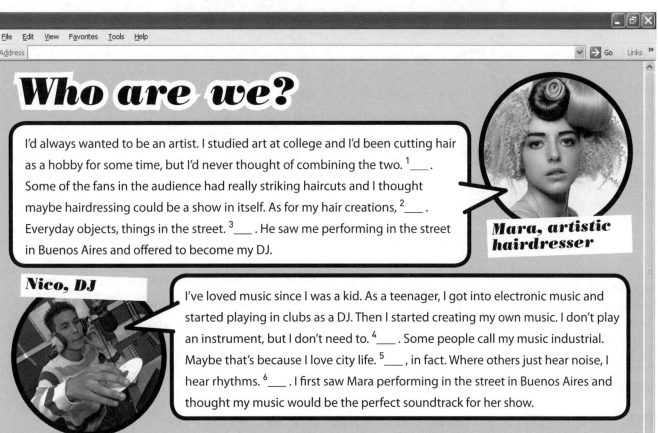

File  Edit  View  Favorites  Tools  Help

Address

# Who are we?

I'd always wanted to be an artist. I studied art at college and I'd been cutting hair as a hobby for some time, but I'd never thought of combining the two. ¹___. Some of the fans in the audience had really striking haircuts and I thought maybe hairdressing could be a show in itself. As for my hair creations, ²___. Everyday objects, things in the street. ³___ . He saw me performing in the street in Buenos Aires and offered to become my DJ.

*Mara, artistic hairdresser*

*Nico, DJ*

I've loved music since I was a kid. As a teenager, I got into electronic music and started playing in clubs as a DJ. Then I started creating my own music. I don't play an instrument, but I don't need to. ⁴___ . Some people call my music industrial. Maybe that's because I love city life. ⁵___ , in fact. Where others just hear noise, I hear rhythms. ⁶___ . I first saw Mara performing in the street in Buenos Aires and thought my music would be the perfect soundtrack for her show.

GRAMMAR

Describing
scenes:
present and
past participle
clauses

**4** Look at these descriptions of some famous things. Rewrite each pair of sentences as a single sentence using present or past participle clauses.

1 It's a statue of a woman. She's holding a torch.

_____

2 It's a collection of short stories. They were written in Arabic.

_____

3 It's a film about an ex-CIA secret operative. He's running from the CIA.

_____

4 It's a book about a sailor. He's hunting a white whale.

_____

5 It's a building in India. It's made of white marble.

_____

6 It's a painting of stars. The stars are shining in the night sky.

_____

Can you identify the things in the descriptions? Write your answers and then check in the box on the left.

1 _____  4 _____

2 _____  5 _____

3 _____  6 _____

Vincent Van Gogh
Mahal  6 Starry Night, by
Herman Melville  5 The Taj
Identity  4 Moby Dick, by
Nights  3 The Bourne
2 One Thousand and One
1 The Statue of Liberty

**5** Complete these two descriptions of dreams from an internet dream interpretation website using the correct form of the verbs in the box. Use each verb once.

beat   call   chase   cover   go   hide   make   move   take   wait

http://www.YourDreams.com

Find out what your dreams mean at **YourDreams.com**

**ScotsKev**

I was in the street of a city I didn't recognise. Suddenly I heard someone behind me ¹_____ my name, and when I turned round, I saw a man ²_____ me, his face ³_____ behind a carnival mask. I started running and saw a queue of people ⁴_____ at a bus stop.

I asked for help, but nobody listened. Then I noticed that the people were all carrying objects ⁵_____ from my flat. I tried to take back my laptop, but the person pushed me over. At that point I woke up.

Can anybody suggest what this might mean?

**Adeleh1984**

I was walking across a field ⁶_____ in tall grass when I became aware of something ⁷_____ in the air above me. I looked up and saw that there was a bird ⁸_____ round in circles over my head. It was so low now that I could hear its wings ⁹_____ in the warm air. It was then that I noticed it was carrying something ¹⁰_____ of gold in its beak. I jumped up to try and get it and to my amazement, I found I could follow the bird as it flew away. I was flying! What does this dream tell me?

## Over to you

Do you think dreams have a meaning? Have you had any interesting dreams? What happened?

## VOCABULARY

Discussing possible solutions

**6** Complete the conversation using the words in the box.

alternatively   another   approach   considering   different   feasible   practical   recommend   something   tricky   worth   wouldn't

TONI   What's up? You look stressed out.

KIM   It's Jacob. I think he's doing too much private work in company time.

TONI   It might be ¹_____ talking to him.

KIM   That would be ²_____. I mean, I don't have any evidence.

LEA   ³_____ option would be to give him deadlines for all the work he does.

KIM   It's worth ⁴_____, but we've always worked on trust. It creates a good atmosphere.

TONI   Who sits next to him? Jan, right? A ⁵_____ ⁶_____ would be to get her to keep an eye on what he's doing.

KIM   That's not really ⁷_____. Jan's got a lot of her own work to do.

LEA   And I ⁸_____ ⁹_____ spying on him – he'd take that really badly.

TONI   ¹⁰_____, you could establish a timetable with him. Tell him that you need to know when he's doing company work so you can co-ordinate things.

LEA   That's quite ¹¹_____.

KIM   Yes, there's ¹²_____ in that, I agree. It brings up the issue, but without accusing him directly.

# EXPLOREWriting

7 Read part of an email in which someone asks a friend for advice about a problem at work. What advice would you give the person?

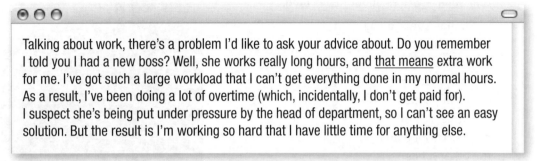

Talking about work, there's a problem I'd like to ask your advice about. Do you remember I told you I had a new boss? Well, she works really long hours, and <u>that means</u> extra work for me. I've got such a large workload that I can't get everything done in my normal hours. As a result, I've been doing a lot of overtime (which, incidentally, I don't get paid for). I suspect she's being put under pressure by the head of department, so I can't see an easy solution. But the result is I'm working so hard that I have little time for anything else.

8 Read the friend's response. Does the advice coincide with your ideas?

<u>It sounds to me like</u> your boss is a workaholic, which is a real problem if, as you suggest, she's under pressure from above to get things done. Am I right in thinking that she's not very approachable? I imagine you'd have said something to her if she was. My feeling is that you have two choices. Either you accept your working hours and ask to be paid for overtime, or you need to explain that you've got more work than you can cope with. Either way, you need to talk to your boss. I'd be tempted to explain the situation in an email first, and arrange to talk about it. Who knows, she might be completely unaware of your situation.

9 Read the first email again. <u>Underline</u> five more words or expressions that the writer uses to talk about the consequences of the problem. Write them in this list.

1 *that means*
2 _____ + noun phrase + _____
3 _____  _____  _____
4 _____
5 _____  _____  _____
6 _____ + adjective + _____

10 Choose the best option to describe the friend's analysis of the problem and advice.

a Decisive – she's sure her analysis and advice are right.
b Tentative – she's not sure if her analysis and advice are right.

11 <u>Underline</u> six more expressions in the response that show a tentative approach to analysing the problem and giving advice.

12 Complete this email with words and expressions from Exercise 9. Use a different expression each time.

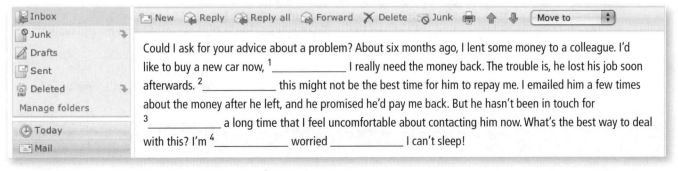

Inbox
Junk
Drafts
Sent
Deleted
Manage folders
Today
Mail

New  Reply  Reply all  Forward  Delete  Junk  Move to

Could I ask for your advice about a problem? About six months ago, I lent some money to a colleague. I'd like to buy a new car now, [1]_____ I really need the money back. The trouble is, he lost his job soon afterwards. [2]_____ this might not be the best time for him to repay me. I emailed him a few times about the money after he left, and he promised he'd pay me back. But he hasn't been in touch for [3]_____ a long time that I feel uncomfortable about contacting him now. What's the best way to deal with this? I'm [4]_____ worried _____ I can't sleep!

13 Write a response to the email giving advice. Be tentative about your analysis of the problem and the advice you include.

**1** Before you watch, think about these questions.

Do you ever read blogs? If so, what blogs do you read, and why do you read them? If not, why not?

**2** Watch the video and tick (✓) the things that Valerie writes about in her blog.

a things she is doing ☐
b bars and restaurants ☐
c the news ☐
d the weather ☐
e local politics ☐
f films ☐
g her travel plans ☐
h other blogs ☐
i games she plays ☐

Valerie

**3** Watch again and (circle) the best option to complete the sentences.

1 Valerie calls herself a Francunian because …
   a it's the way people from Manchester refer to French people.
   b it's the English word for a person from Manchester.
   c it's a combination she has invented of the words French and Mancunian.
2 What she writes about …
   a always stays the same.
   b changes all the time.
   c depends on the weather.
3 She writes in her blog …
   a more often some months than others.
   b once a day.
   c only when she feels strongly about something.
4 A possible plan she has is to …
   a become a professional writer.
   b publish her blog as a book.
   c include more humour in her blog.

**4** Complete the sentences. Then watch again to check.

1 She mainly writes her blog for _____ .
2 Her blog isn't a 'flat' thing, it _____ .
3 The interview with Valerie took place in _____ .
4 This month, she has drawn inspiration from a poem she saw on _____ .
5 If her blog became a book, she would call it _____ .

**5** Valerie is an excellent non-native speaker and makes very few mistakes. Can you find and correct *two* mistakes related to the underlined relative pronouns in these extracts?

1 Basically, my inspiration comes from a lot of, erm, different activities <u>which</u> I do.
2 It's like a blank canvas <u>where</u> I write about all sorts of things.
3 It's a bit of an informal website <u>when</u> you can get some information for what's happening.
4 I linked it to a lovely Mancunian poet called Lemn Sissay <u>which</u> has a nice poem written on the wall in Manchester <u>which</u> ends up talking about rainbows, <u>which</u> I really like.
5 You never know <u>how</u> it could happen.

**6** Imagine that you decide to start a blog, or start a new one if you already write one. What will your blog be about? Who will you want to read your blog?

## GLOSSARY

**canvas** (noun): strong cloth used for painting
**blank** (adjective): empty

# Unit 1

1 2 self-esteem   3 a lot of practice   4 your interests
5 the will to succeed   6 training   7 specific goals
8 feedback   9 results   10 experience

2 2 saying anything new   3 logical   4 makes; sense
5 convinced   6 persuasive   7 hard; follow   8 don't get
9 simplistic   10 whole picture

3 2 've/have spoken / been speaking   3 have worked
4 haven't/have not lived / been living   5 's/has helped
6 've/have earned / been earning   7 have you ever wanted
8 's/has been preparing

4 2 endurance   3 reflexes   4 balance   5 eyesight   6 numbers
7 logically   8 focused   9 well-organised   10 self-disciplined
11 communicator   12 compromise   13 delegate   14 manage
15 sensitive

5 2 g   3 a   4 e   5 i   6 b   7 f   8 c   9 h

6 It's for people who want to write and sing their own songs.

9 b ✓   c ✓   d ✓   e ✓   f ✓   g ✓

10 **I am** writing in response to **your** advert … (Paragraph 1)
… has allowed me **to** develop the skills … (Paragraph 3)
**I am** a good communicator … (Paragraph 3)
**I have** been unemployed since … (Paragraph 3)
**I am** sure this would be useful … (Paragraph 3)
Thank you in advance **for** considering my application. (Paragraph 4)
… and look forward to hearing **from** you … (Paragraph 4)

## INTERVIEW Hidden talents

2 Clare: cake decorating / Yes
Carlos: writing / Yes

3 1 About three years ago.
2 She goes to college one night a week.
3 birthday cakes, wedding cakes, christening cakes, cakes for hen parties
4 A wedding cake, because it was quite a complex design / it had quite delicate flowers.

4 1 took up   2 do actually   3 so far   4 all sorts   5 takes up

5 1 F (He doesn't remember exactly when he started.)
2 F (He learned to find this at school.)
3 T
4 T
5 F (He separated the story into three points of view.)
6 F (It was as a result of presenting the novel in a contest.)

6 Meaningful collocations are: apply to a school; express yourself; study a novel / skills / techniques; improve a novel / skills / yourself / a school / techniques; publish a novel / yourself
Carlos uses: apply to a school, express yourself, study techniques, improve skills, publish a novel

# Unit 2

1 b I told her I'd nearly finished it
c that explains it
d I thought you'd done that report
e Another option is to text everyone
f The logical thing is to print it out
g she told me you'd sent us all a copy
h What if I send it now
i That's not what she said

2 g   3 b   4 a   5 i   6 c   7 h   8 f   9 e

2 2 It had already finished when he heard about it.
3 He didn't read my email … because he'd been away for a few days.
4 By the time they contacted us we'd sold it.
5 We assumed they'd decided not to buy it.
6 When I got to the station my train had already left.
7 Then I realised I'd taken the wrong one.
8 nobody noticed that I hadn't arrived on time.

3 1 'd/had been   2 'd/had reserved   3 got out   4 handed
5 'd/had printed out   6 hadn't/had not booked   7 explained
8 'd/had slept   9 told   10 had taken

4 1 carelessly   2 gradually   3 reluctantly / enthusiastically
4 deliberately / accidentally   5 calmly / furiously

5 1 enthusiastically   2 reluctantly   3 carefully   4 carelessly
5 suddenly   6 gradually   7 deliberately   8 accidentally
9 furiously   10 calmly

6 1 Enthusiastically I suggested / I suggested enthusiastically
2 We carefully selected / We selected carefully
3 Eventually people started / People eventually started

7 1 was returning   2 'd been cutting down   3 was resting
4 had been calling   5 was still sitting   6 had been carrying

8 1 became   2 had been killing   3 was hiding   4 finally got
5 had been trying   6 had taken   7 created   8 had been fighting
9 were looking

9 1 was told   2 said they'd   3 would   4 still hadn't   5 I'd been
6 they'd already   7 they said   8 had   9 go to the trouble of
10 ended up   11 That cost me

12 a 4   b 7   c 3   d 8   e 5   f 1   g 6   h 2

13 take care of it, put an end to, deal with it, sort the problem out

14 1 predicament   2 cut off   3 overdue   4 debt   5 statement
6 bounced   7 file; claim   8 harassment

## INTERVIEW A holiday to forget

2 Emma: 2 and 5

3 When Emma was seven years old she went on a caravan holiday with ~~six~~ *seven* other people. They set off in two cars, and an hour ~~later~~ *before they arrived* one of the children was sick, so they had to stop to clean up. By ~~the time they arrived at the caravan site~~ *four o´clock the following morning*, six people in the group had the sickness bug, and by the end of the holiday, everyone in the group had had it. While they were there, the people who were well slept in ~~the~~ *one* caravan, and those who were ill slept in ~~a house~~ *the other one*.

4 1 get   2 get   3 get   4 get; getting   5 got

5 1 Two weeks
2 Because the town they were going to had a beach.
3 She was frightened that Emma's car was going to crash into hers.

6 1 *Steep* means *rising at a sharp angle*, and Emma describes the hill as 'one of the steepest hills in England'.
2 A *banger* is a very old car in bad condition. She describes her car as 'an old banger of a car'.
3 *Grab* means to take hold of something suddenly or roughly. Her friend *grabbed* a cushion to cover her face.
4 *Petrified* means *extremely frightened*. Her friend was *petrified* in the car behind hers.
5 *Smash into* means hit with great force, causing damage. Her friend thought Emma's car was going to *smash into* hers.
6 *Leap* means *make a large jump or sudden movement*. The three men *leapt out* of their cars to help them.

## Unit 3

**1**  2 like the sound of   3 like to give; a try   4 narrowed it down to
5 it's a choice between; or   6 be happy with either
7 can't make up her mind   8 in two minds about
9 got mixed feelings about   10 isn't really my thing
11 There's no way I'm   12 doesn't really appeal to me

**2**  1 give up   2 signed up
3 carry on (*keep on* is possible, but *keep* is needed in number 4)
4 keep up   5 drop out   6 take on   7 work on   8 sign up
9 work towards   10 carry on

**3**  **Across**

1 evening   4 on-campus   10 seminar   11 face-to-face
13 lecture   14 final exam   16 postgraduate
17 full-time   18 online

**Down**

2 vocational   3 assignment   5 experience   6 coursework
7 apprenticeship   8 distance   9 dissertation   12 hands-on
15 part-time

**4**  1 are always getting   2 both are possible   3 hardly ever come
4 suffers   5 both are possible   6 thought
7 both are possible   8 both are possible   9 both are possible

**5**  1 did your family use to live   2 Was the weather
3 would you and your friends play
4 does your family eat / will your family eat
5 do you do / will you do   6 Are you always sending

**6**  1 was one of those people who   2 He'd always
3 I've never known anybody/anyone so
4 was a really positive influence on
5 was the most positive person I've/I'd ever met
6 would never   7 made a very big impression on
8 taught me a lot about   9 owe

**8**  c

**9**  c

**10**  1 always, invariably, constantly   2 just how much, far more
3 my own school days, in those days, Nowadays, the days when
4 rightly   5 surely   6 timely

### INTERVIEW Pass it on

**2**  Carlos' work: football coaching
Liu's work: teaching Chinese, art and handcraft
They both teach something to children.

**3**  pass C   brush pen L   dribble C   ink drawings L
1 dribble/control   2 pass   3 ink drawing   4 brush pen

**4**  1 community   2 Victoria   3 hard; challenge   4 developing

**5**  1 When she was four years old, on the walls (of her house).
2 No, they didn't (she says they didn't tell her off). They sent her to art school.
3 Art and Design.
4 She studied for a degree in architecture at Liverpool University.
5 In Manchester.
6 Their names in Chinese.

## Unit 4

**1**  1 realistic   2 amuse   3 make people think   4 signify
5 monuments   6 commemorate   7 traditional   8 honour
9 abstract   10 modern   11 sculpture
12 statues   13 celebrates

**2**  1 erected   2 a big impression   3 a tourist attraction
4 to make of it   5 a lot of controversy   6 heavily criticised
7 an eyesore   8 to love it   9 a landmark   10 the urban landscape

**3**  1 was put up   2 was badly received by   3 were baffled by
4 warmed to

**4**  1 he was probably the most famous / he probably was the most famous
2 he had his first breakthrough
3 His first single came out
4 One of his techniques was
He was Jimi Hendrix.
5 she started out as a nurse
6 she had her first real success
7 One of her most famous works is
8 she won a Grand Masters Award for
She was Agatha Christie.

**5**  1 made   2 was known   3 was taken   4 encouraged   5 came
6 was invited   7 wasn't received   8 left   9 was given
10 has not been forgotten   11 was named   12 be seen

**6**  1 is known   2 is said   3 can be found   4 was published
5 It is estimated   6 is still read   7 have been published

**7**  1 think; right; saying   2 heard that   3 They say
4 remember rightly   5 read somewhere
6 far as; remember/recall

**8**  1 c   2 h   3 e   4 a   5 d   6 j   7 f   8 i   9 g   10 b

**9 & 10**  1 Peru
2 the Incas
3 It was built in the 15$^{th}$ century, and so is somewhere between 500 and 600 years old. (This is not answered on the website.)
4 1911
5 Hawaiian-born explorer Hiram Bingham

**11**  1 T
2 F (It had never been lost to those who lived around it.)
3 F (Bingham didn't find Machu Picchu, he was taken to it.)
4 T
5 T
6 F (Other people had grown crops at Machu Picchu before the peasant farmers that Bingham met.)

**12**  1 remarkable   2 the Conquest   3 colonial rule
4 stumbled upon   5 Quechua   6 ruins   7 granite   8 masonry

**13**  Suggested answers:
1 The ruins at Machu Picchu are very big and impressive, so it's surprising that the Spanish didn't find them during hundreds of years of colonial rule.
2 The writer is saying that Bingham didn't discover Machu Picchu because local people always knew it was there. However, unlike Bingham, the local people had no way of telling the rest of the world about it.

### INTERVIEW Come to my country

**2**  Rezarta comes from Albania. She mentions the Ionian Sea and the Adriatic.
Liu comes from China. She mentions Beijing and the Forbidden City.

**3**  1 L   2 R   3 R   4 R   5 BOTH   6 R   7 L   8 R

**4**  1 unknown   2 undergone   3 point   4 encourage   5 pleasantly
6 experience

**5**  1 F (He's flying from Australia.)   2 F (He has never been before.)
3 T   4 F (Liu's going to take him to her hometown to meet them after being in Beijing.)   5 T

**6**  b

# Unit 5

**1** 1 portrays 2 seems 3 implies 4 highlights

**2** 1 seems 2 highlights 3 implies 4 portrays

**3** 1 can't see 2 shape 3 size 4 style 5 colours 6 nice
7 make; feel 8 would look 9 could go 10 can/could imagine
11 wouldn't suit 12 could put

**4** 2 environmentally 3 attractive; aesthetic
4 long-lasting; durable 5 novel; innovative 6 straightforward
7 meaningful; purposeful

**5** a 2 b 4 c 6 d 3 e 5 f 7 g 1

**6** The zip, ~~which is~~ known as a zipper in US English, is a fastening
device ~~that is~~ used on clothes, bags and camping equipment. ~~It was~~
first patented in 1891, ~~but~~ it didn't become a practical alternative
to buttons until years later. Early versions, ~~which were~~ made only
of metal, used hooks and eyes, but they came apart easily. A zipper
~~that was~~ based on interlocking teeth was invented by the Swedish
engineer Gideon Sundback in 1914, and this is the system ~~that is~~ used
in zips around the world today.

**7** 1 The World Wide Web, used by millions of people around the
globe, is considered a design classic.
3 Developed in 1990 by Tim Berners-Lee, the Web revolutionised
our search for information.
5 The first-ever web browser, called the World Wide Web, couldn't
show graphics in web pages.

**8** Suggested answers:
1 First launched in 1985, it's an operating system installed on
millions of computers. Product: Microsoft Windows
2 This object, called a *biro* in English, is a popular pen invented by
a Hungarian newspaper editor. Product: ballpoint pen
3 Designed by Harry Beck in 1931, this map was a revolutionary
concept, used today by transport systems around the world.
Product: the London Underground (Tube) map

**9** 2 Let's eliminate 3 we all agreed on 4 are out
5 Would that work for 6 all in favour of
7 to change your mind 8 going with

**11** the iPhone

**12** is it
1 can; YouTube 2 is; Wikipedia 3 does; Skype

**13** 1 For instance, such as, like, For example
2 which has revolutionised the way we look for information; which
have helped millions of people to keep in touch with friends –
and make new ones; which means you can easily teach yourself
to use it
3 designed for people (like me) who are not really into technology

## DOCUMENTARY The sculptors

**1** 1 They are all occupations. *Student* could be different because it
isn't a paid occupation.
2 They are all types of or examples of art. *Sculpture* could be
different because the others are all two-dimensional.
3 They are all materials. *Papier-mâché* could be different because
it's paper, whereas the others are metal or made of metal. *Metal*
could also be different because the others are material in a
particular form, and not a primary material.
4 The verbs all refer to the way things are connected. *Cut* could be
the different one because it refers to separating, and not joining,
things.
5 They all refer to the form of an object. *Bit* could be the different
one because it refers to a small piece of something and the
other words refer to its overall form.

**2** 1 sculpture (*shape*, *structure* and *metal* are also possible)
2 weld (*sculptor* and *metal* are also possible)
3 cut (*sculptor* and *metal* are also possible)

**3** 1 Jayne 2 Tony 3 Both 4 Tony 5 Both

**4** 1 F (He moved to Cambridge from Birmingham.)
2 F (He retired as a university lecturer about ten years ago.)
3 F (He has been painting and drawing his whole life.)
4 T
5 F (He and his wife cycled about a thousand miles on it.)
6 T (He wanted her to make something with him.)

**5** Age: 37
Family: two children
Studies: she studied illustration
First profession: she became a social worker
How she got into sculpting: she saw some of Tony's sculptures and
contacted him

**6** Step 1: He makes a very small drawing of the sculpture.
Step 2: He bends the rod into the shape he needs.
Step 3: He joins the bits of rod together by welding them.

**7** 1 How to break down the process of making a sculpture into
manageable pieces.
2 He worked alone.
3 You can share the enjoyment of the creative process with
someone else.
4 He's kind, gentle, patient, gives clear explanations, and is
positive and encouraging.
5 That art is about people, community and an enjoyment of life.
6 Jayne wants to make some money from her work, and Tony
gives his work to public places.
7 Stimulate people, give people an enjoyment of life and bring
people together.
8 A supply of metal, his time and his expertise. Because this has
given her the opportunity to start a career as a sculptor.

**8** 1 going to be the next one 2 to produce perfection
3 a little boy and his grandad
4 an adult taking the child seriously as a person

**9** 1 into; back 2 up; back into; out for 3 together 4 down
5 out 6 out; out; together

# Unit 6

1  1 be suspected   2 be arrested   3 be accused   4 be sentenced
   5 go to prison

2  1 fine   2 law   3 arrested   4 suspected   5 accused
   6 sentenced   7 community   8 prison   9 sentence

3  1 Include letters and numbers. **That way,** your password will
     be harder to guess. / Include letters and numbers. **Then** your
     password will be harder to guess.
   2 Change your password regularly. **Otherwise,** someone could
     see and remember it. / Change your password regularly, **or else**
     someone could see and remember it.
   3 Memorise and destroy your password. **Then** nobody will find it. /
     Memorise and destroy your password. **That way,** nobody will find it.
   4 It's important to sign out after every session, **or** others could
     access your information. / It's important to sign out after every
     session. **If not,** others could access your information.

4  2 They'll tell you that
   3 As far as they're concerned
   4 There's also the argument that
   5 On the other hand, you have people who say that
   6 Many new groups will say that
   7 What they say is that
   8 A lot of people think that / People think that a lot of

5  2 a, b, d   3 e   4 c   5 a, b, d

6  Suggested answers:
   1 If someone is caught sharing files online, they should lose their
     internet connection.
   2 I wouldn't watch an illegal copy of a film even if a friend gave it to
     me.
   3 People will / would pay to read online newspapers as long as
     the cost is / was reasonable.
   4 I won't / wouldn't upgrade my computer unless my current one
     stops / stopped working.
   5 I'd do / I'll do all my banking on the Internet provided it was / is
     completely safe.

7  1 b   2 e   3 a   4 extra verb   5 d   6 c

8  1 move/shift   2 link/connect   3 swap/switch   4 leave
   5 place/stick   6 cut/drop

9  1 If it's   2 I'll probably   3 if it's   4 I'll definitely   5 if
   6 wouldn't dream of   7 There's no way I'd   8 I'd always
   9 If you   10 really important   11 increasingly common
   12 the proper thing to do   13 unheard of   14 expected to

10 1 Suggested answer: Computer hacking involves getting into
     someone else's computer system without permission in order to
     find out information or do something illegal.

12 Suggested answers:
   1 Because they allow them to do training courses in ethical
     hacking without having to take time off work.
   2 You can study it four ways: in a classroom, studying online,
     offline with study materials, and using mobile phone downloads
     – the last three ways are relatively new.
   3 An increase in the number of news stories about hacking and its
     inclusion in popular TV series.
   4 The fact that they work very quickly and are able to steal data
     without you knowing about it.
   5 They both know how to break into computer systems, how to
     make computer viruses, and how social engineering works.
   6 They hope to get an official qualification in ethical hacking.
     This qualification is important because it has the support of the
     industry's most important organisation.
   7 Because the skills students learn could be used for illegal
     purposes.
   8 They all work for a legitimate company.

13 a 4   b 3   c 2   d 1

14 1 on the rise   2 in the workplace   3 on the move
   4 in constant demand   5 in employment   6 in the field

## INTERVIEW Virtual world

2  1 Qusay   2 Neither speaker   3 Qusay   4 Neither speaker

3  They both talk about special clothes, but Qusay talks about real
   clothes, and Ekapop talks about clothes you can buy in a virtual
   online world.

4  1 impact   2 window   3 activities   4 wedding
   5 dress   6 design

5  1 As part of a research project organised by a friend on his
     master's course.
   2 They buy their character online.
   3 They walk around, interact with other users, shop and view
     products in different stores.
   4 Because more and more users are taking part in it.
   5 He didn't spend any money on clothes.
   6 Because they want to look different from the other people in
     Second Life.

6  1 c   2 e   3 a   4 b   5 d

# Unit 7

1  1 solve   2 ignore it   3 mull over   4 sorting out   5 put off
   6 come up with   7 finding the answer to   8 concentrate on it
   9 work out   10 give up on it   11 tackle it   12 figured out

2  1 biggest ('big' would also be possible) problem was
   2 found it; difficult   3 presented me with
   4 what; decided; do was   5 way of solving   6 What; learned was

3  First part:   1 c   2 d   3 a   4 f   5 b   6 e
   Second part:   1 3   2 6   3 5   4 2   5 1   6 4

4  1 It's a statue of a woman holding a torch.
   2 It's a collection of short stories written in Arabic.
   3 It's a film about an ex-CIA secret operative running from the CIA.
   4 It's a book about a sailor hunting a white whale.
   5 It's a building in India made of white marble.
   6 It's a painting of stars shining in the night sky.

5  1 calling   2 chasing   3 hidden   4 waiting   5 taken   6 covered
   7 moving   8 going   9 beating   10 made

6  1 worth   2 tricky   3 Another   4 considering   5 different
   6 approach   7 practical   8 wouldn't   9 recommend
   10 Alternatively   11 feasible   12 something

9  2 such + noun phrase + that   3 As a result   4 so
   5 the result is   6 so + adjective + that

10 b

11 as you suggest; Am I right in thinking; I imagine; My feeling is; I'd
   be tempted to; Who knows, she might

12 1 so   2 That means / As a result, / The result is   3 such   4 so;
   that

## INTERVIEW An inspired blog

2  a ✓   b ✓   c ✓   d ✓   g ✓

3  1 c   2 b   3 a   4 b

4  1 Mancunians   2 evolves all the time   3 November
   4 a wall in Manchester (in Oxford Road)
   5 Memoirs of a Francunian

5  The corrected errors are:
   3 It's a bit of an informal website **where** you can get some
     information for what's happening.
   4 I linked it to a lovely Mancunian poet called Lemn Sissay **who**
     has a nice poem written on the wall in Manchester …

# Unit 8

**1**   1 may/might/could   2 can't/couldn't   3 must
   4 may/could/might   5 couldn't/can't
   6 may/might/could   7 must

**2**   1 They may/might/could have abandoned the ship in search of provisions.
   2 It can't/couldn't have been the result of a pirate attack.
   3 But they might/could/may well have left the ship through fear of an explosion.
   4 The people on board must have been abducted by aliens.
   5 They couldn't/can't have died out slowly.
   6 If so, the asteroid must have been enormous
   7 An asteroid might/could/may well have caused the dinosaurs to die out.
   8 They could/might/may have been wiped out by a massive volcanic eruption.

**3**   1 fascinated, intrigued   2 out of place, isolated
   3 horrified, appalled   4 baffled, mystified
   5 humiliated, mortified   6 thrilled, delighted

**4**   1 fascinated   2 delighted   3 thrilled   4 appalled/horrified
   5 intrigued   6 horrified/appalled   7 out of place   8 isolated
   9 mortified   10 humiliated

**5**   1 regret   2 glad / not sorry   3 wish   4 sorry
   5 not sorry / glad   6 don't regret   7 If only   8 a good thing

**6**   2 If you hadn't lent me your newspaper, I wouldn't have seen that job ad.
   3 I'd be working as a security guard if I hadn't applied for the job.
   4 If James had asked her to marry him, she'd have said yes.
   5 If they'd been married, she wouldn't have moved to Australia.
   6 She wouldn't be living by a beach now if she'd stayed in the UK.

**7**   1 would have told   2 would have seen   3 wouldn't have lied
   4 would have heard   5 would have found   6 wouldn't have taken

**8**   1 mother tongue   2 official language   3 first language
   4 dialect   5 second language   6 common language
   7 accent   8 multilingual   9 bilingual   10 regional language

**9**   1 mobile phone (UK) / cell phone (US)
   2 pavement (UK) / sidewalk (US)
   3 underground (UK) / subway (US)
   4 favourite (UK) / favorite (US)
   5 behaviour (UK) / behavior (US)

**12**   b

**13**   1 a   2 a   3 b   4 b   5 a   6 b

**14**   2 the banging sound of civility's **bar** as it is lowered another notch
   3 they **camp** in the middle of the sidewalk
   4 **funnel** down subway stairs
   5 Once more into the **breach**
   6 perform something akin to **interpretive dance**
   7 transformed into a **Bond-like** instrument of death

**15**   1 to talk a lot   2 a selfish person   3 going up slowly
   4 looking angrily   5 verbally attacked with a lot of rude language
   6 thrown with force   7 to complain

## INTERVIEW Cultural difference

**2**

|   | Aurora | Monica |
|---|---|---|
| 1 | The Caribbean | Spain |
| 2 | Yes, two: hugging and using your nose to indicate puzzlement | Yes, two: eating times and menus for vegetarians |
| 3 | No | Yes |

**3**   1 T   2 F (Photo c shows a hug.)
   3 F (She doesn't hug people so much.)   4 T

**4**   1 a   2 b   3 b   4 a

**5**   1 In a restaurant.
   2 She told a waiter she wanted to have dinner.
   3 The waiter was shocked because in that country it was very late to have dinner.
   4 She noticed the letter 'v' by the name of some of the food items. They indicated which dishes were vegetarian.
   5 She thought it was a nice surprise.

6 Sometimes the restaurants tell you which meals are suitable for vegetarians but on other occasions they are not very helpful in explaining what is suitable, and indeed will have nothing for vegetarians.
   7 He came out of the kitchen to see who was eating so late.

**6**   She starts by saying it was about half past nine, but at the end she says it was half past ten.

**7**   1 usual   2 sometimes   3 find   4 will have   5 will not explain

# Unit 9

**1**   1 through   2 off   3 into   4 along (through is also possible but is needed in number 1)   5 onto   6 from   7 over   8 up   9 together

**2**   1 put their stories onto   2 both are possible
   3 goes along a digital cable   4 turns the file into
   5 exposes the film onto   6 cuts the contents onto the plastic
   7 prints the newspaper onto   8 goes into the press
   9 emerges from the press   10 cut the sheets into
   11 both are possible   12 both are possible

**3**   a Once this is done   b You remember I told you about
   c The first thing is   d And that's the whole process
   e The next step is   f I'll explain that in a minute
   g What happens next is

**4**   2 f   3 a/e/g   4 a/e/g   5 a/e/g   6 b   7 d

**5**   1 Following that (3, 4 or 5)   2 First of all (1)
   3 Earlier I mentioned (6)   4 To start off (1)
   5 After that (3, 4 or 5)   6 And that's it (7)
   7 To begin with (1)   8 I'll come back to that later (2)

**6**   1 duties   2 supervising   3 answer / report   4 task / responsibility
   5 responsibility / task   6 manage / oversee
   7 oversee / manage   8 accountable   9 charge   10 up
   11 report / answer   12 responsible

**7**   1 d   2 e   3 a   4 h   5 g   6 f   7 c   8 b

**8**   1 be looking; main areas   2 Let's begin   3 all; wanted; say
   4 Next; like to say something   5 it; far as; concerned
   6 Let's move on   7 OK, that's

**9**   1 I'd like to talk about three main things.
   2 I've divided my talk into three parts.
   3 The next thing is its history.
   4 Now let's take a look at its history.
   5 So, we've talked about how we play the music.

**11**   The note gives a complete answer to questions 1, 2 and 4.
   It gives an incomplete answer to questions 3 (it's not clear if there are other responsibilities) and 7 (it doesn't say how to contact Jo, the office manager).
   It doesn't answer questions 5 and 6.

**12**   1 detailing   2 don't hesitate   3 include   4 take you
   5 you'll find   6 doubts

## DOCUMENTARY The human rights lawyer

**2**   1 General Assembly   2 Security Council   3 Court of Justice
   4 Children's   5 Development

**3**   1 International Court of Justice   2 General Assembly
   3 Children's Fund (UNICEF)   4 High Commission for Refugees
   5 Development Programme (UNDP)   6 Security Council

**4**   1 a lecturer (at the University of Cambridge) and as a barrister.
   2 Public International Law.
   3 woman judge of the International Court of Justice.
   4 the United Nations.
   5 every state in the world.

**5**   1 The decision to explore his field in a more practical sense / see international law in action.
   2 He did research on the condition of refugees.
   3 To investigate whether refugees enjoyed their fundamental rights in countries of asylum.
   4 In two refugee camps in Kenya.

**6**   a

**7**   1 weaker   2 less   3 a lot of   4 accountability

**8**   1 c   2 f   3 b   4 g   5 a   6 d   7 e

# Unit 10

**1** 1 discovered  2 located  3 reached  4 scanned  5 search for
6 detected  7 doing research into  8 map  9 explore
10 found evidence of

**2** 1 us to  2 would; on  3 would; no word necessary  4 is; for
5 us; to  6 would; no word necessary  7 is; for  8 would; of; to
9 us to  10 is; for

**3** 1 think; getting; going  2 spend; doing  3 to do; make
4 interested; learning  5 do; work  6 make; studying
7 causing; understand  8 Putting; to succeed
9 challenging; facing

**4** ... I'm **planning** to spend a year **travelling** around Europe. But I
also want to do something that doesn't only involve **visiting** nice
places. I've been **doing** some research on the Internet and I think
voluntary work would be an **interesting** thing to do. ... I wouldn't
want to spend so much time away from home without **bringing**
something back with me, so after **gaining** some experience,
maybe organic **farming** is an area I could work in back home. ...

**5** 1 b  2 e  3 a  4 c  5 d  6 i  7 f  8 j  9 g  10 h

**6** 2 Depending on who you ask
3 According to Son House's version
4 In other sources it claims that
5 his death certificate makes no mention of this
6 All sources are in agreement that

**7** 1 free to  2 freedom to / right to  3 option of
4 right to / freedom to  5 obliged to
6 compulsory; to  7 expected to  8 duty to

**8** 1 d  2 a  3 b  4 e  5 c

**9** a

**10** Sentences 5 and 6 are not true. Space exploration is for economic
benefit, and a return trip to the nearest star to our solar system is
not feasible today.

**11** Suggested answers:
1 Very popular. He says there would be no shortage of volunteers.
2 He compares one-way space travel to people crossing oceans to
discover new countries.
3 To use the moon as a permanent base for travel to other places.
4 He's referring to using spacecraft with people on board for
missions.
5 That children born on the spacecraft would have to continue the
mission.
6 Building more powerful telescopes.

**12** 1 b  2 a  3 b  4 a  5 b  6 b

## INTERVIEW Environmental issues

**2** Liu mentions changes to transportation and the way her city looks.
Adriana mentions energy use and production, and the
environment.

**3** 1 She's been back three times.
2 In her hometown and the whole of China.
3 Higher buildings, more cars and fewer bicycles.
4 They make people's lives more convenient.
5 They have cut down the trees along an avenue where she used
to ride her bicycle.
6 Fifty years old or more.

**4** 1 how  2 get; rather  3 used to  4 broadened  5 all gone

**5** 1 working  2 reduce  3 depends  4 smaller  5 less; less
6 normally

**6** 1 /s/  2 /z/  3 /ʒ/  4 /z/

# Unit 11

**1** 1 get the best out of  2 gets; talking  3 manipulate
4 clam up  5 handle  6 puts; on edge  7 put; at ease
8 brings out the worst in

**2** 1 b, e, h  2 d, i, k  3 a, c, j  4 f, g, l

**3** 2 (C) promised  3 (I) admitted  4 (C) complained
5 (I) challenged  6 (I) threatened  7 (C) refused
8 (C) announced  9 (I) advised  10 (C) thanked

**4** 1 b  2 a, b  3 c  4 a, c  5 a, b  6 b  7 a, b  8 b

**5** 1 she challenged me to a game of chess
2 I told her (that) I don't/didn't play well / she promised not to
play her best
3 a friend admitted (to) losing a book I lent him / admitted (that)
he'd lost a book I lent him
4 I apologised for my angry reaction
5 my sister announced (that) she's / she was getting married
6 asked me to take photos at the wedding
7 asked to see my identification
8 He threatened to arrest me

**6** 1 d  2 a  3 d  4 b  5 c  6 d

**7** 2 most  3 just over half  4 just under a quarter
5 none  6 almost none  7 nearly all  8 four out of ten
9 about a third  10 a fifth

**8** 1 Socialists  2 Conservatives  3 Liberals  4 Greens
5 Undecided

**9** 1 certainly due  2 suggests  3 perhaps  4 reveal
5 look unlikely  6 would seem

**10** Suggested answer:
The figures show the results of the final opinion poll before the
September elections.
The first thing that stands out is that there has been a sharp
increase in the popularity of the Conservatives. This reveals
that people now see them as the best party to lead the local
government. It is a significant change because the percentage of
voters who favour the Socialists has also risen, although support
for them hasn't reached its April high point. This would seem to
indicate that Socialist voters are gradually forgetting about their
financial scandals. Another dramatic change is the fall in the
number of undecided voters. This is almost certainly due to the
elections being so close, so people have made a decision about
who to vote for.
As for the smaller parties, support for the Greens has fallen to
April levels, whereas votes for the Liberals have gone up slightly.
This is perhaps because some disenchanted Socialist voters
who were undecided in July have decided to vote for the Liberals
instead.
Overall, the results show that Conservatives look very likely to win
the elections. This suggests that the Conservatives' message has
managed to win over the majority of undecided voters.

## INTERVIEW How not to get the job

**3** 1 a  2 b  3 b  4 a  5 b

**4** a 2  b 4  c 3  d 5  e 1

**5** 1 She runs her own company.
2 A lot of people think about what to say but not about the
impression that they give.
3 Looking for poor or homeless people and talking to them to gain
their trust.
4 The ability to understand and appreciate someone else's
situation.
5 Because he was dressed very smartly and this suggested
he wouldn't be able to communicate with poor or homeless
people.
6 Doing dirty and unpleasant activities on a farm.
7 Because she came to the interview dressed very fashionably, in
an extremely short skirt and high-heeled boots.

**6** 1 b  2 e  3 a  4 c  5 d

# Unit 12

**1**  1 Surgery  2 effect  3 Massage  4 symptoms
5 Physiotherapy  6 illness  7 painkiller  8 medicine
9 Acupuncture  10 treatment  11 Hypnosis  12 Side effects
13 remedy  14 antibiotic  15 vaccination  16 placebo

**2**  1 nonsense  2 works  3 effects (*benefit* is also possible here,
but is needed in number 12)  4 nothing  5 believe (*trust* is also
possible here, but is needed in number 9)
6 worthless  7 proof  8 tried  9 trust  10 basis
11 better  12 benefit

**3**  1 'll/will be lying in the sun in the Caribbean.
2 'll/will be analysing last month's sales figures.
3 'll/will be visiting the main sights of the city.
4 'll/will be snowing when you arrive.
5 'll/will be passing through some turbulence.
6 'll/will be sending you a document to translate.
7 'll/will be doing some revision for the exam.

**4**  1 experience is that  2 evidence suggests that
3 For instance  4 always found that
5 research suggests that  6 There's; evidence that
7 for example  8 Experts have shown that
9 give you an example  10 in my experience

**5**  1 I'd reject the proposal on the grounds that it would be expensive.
2 I'd strongly recommend doing it as it would be
3 I'd rule it out because not everyone would enjoy it.
4 I'd advise against it since it would occupy a whole weekend.
5 if I were you, I'd go for it.

**6**  1 treatment  2 health insurance  3 free of charge
4 appointment  5 check-ups  6 high status
7 manner  8 openly  9 entitled  10 access  11 choice
12 people  13 in  14 information  15 out

**8**  1 F (It can be painful, but it's good for your health.)
2 T
3 T
4 F (Laughter is known to release chemicals that make us happy.)

**9**  1 4  2 7  3 3  4 5,6  5 1,6  6 2

**10**  1 c  2 a  3 b  4 b

**11**  1 giggle, guffaw  2 mirth  3 aching, painful  4 accessible
5 turn up  6 wanes  7 emotional  8 outer  9 fake

## INTERVIEW Alternative treatments

**2**

|  | Leo | Anna Laura |
|---|---|---|
| 1 | He hadn't had much experience of it, but he believes in it now. | She was sceptical but is more positive now. |
| 2 | Yes | Yes |
| 3 | Acupuncture | A homeopathic cream |
| 4 | Yes | Yes |

**3**  1 In China.
2 He didn't have much experience of alternative medicine.
3 They wanted to have a baby but couldn't.
4 Because they were disappointed by the help they got from the conventional doctor they went to see.
5 It was possibly caused by stress or hormonal imbalances.
6 He felt nervous and the treatment was painful.

**4**  1 get sick  2 medical check-ups  3 last resort; consult
4 relate; come in  5 course; treatment

**5**  1 T  2 T  3 F (Her sister made her try it.)
4 F (Her husband was bitten.)  5 T
6 F (The symptoms disappeared instantly.)

**6**  1 into  2 about  3 on  4 to  5 to

# Unit 13

**1**  2 get  3 propose  4 make  5 organise  6 propose
7 take  8 organise  9 thrash  10 call  11 talk  12 take

**2**  1 have a word with  2 get everyone's opinion  3 call a meeting
4 make a formal complaint  5 organise a petition
6 organise a demonstration  7 take legal advice
8 take legal action  9 propose a compromise
10 propose an alternative  11 thrash; out  12 talk; over

**3**  1 know  2 afraid  3 besides  4 been  5 thinking  6 about
7 forgetting  8 about  9 any  10 case  11 problem
12 thought  13 about  14 that  15 case

**4**  1 If you ignore a difficult problem, it will usually **go away**.
2 The only way to deal with a difficult problem is to **face up to it**.
3 The key to a successful relationship is learning to **put up with** your partner's annoying habits.
4 To make a relationship work, it's important to **talk over** the things that annoy you.
5 For a new company to work, you just need to **come up with** a good idea.
6 You should always carry out plenty of market research before you consider **setting up** a new company.
7 It's best to leave negotiations for another day if they **break ~~them~~ down**.
8 For negotiations to succeed, it's important to **keep up** the pressure on the other side.

**5**  1 set up  2 brought along  3 talked it over  4 coming up with
5 sort them out  6 break down  7 gone on  8 sit down

**6**  1 gather  2 be compensated for  3 have in mind  4 entitled to
5 honestly see why  6 prepared to  7 afraid we can't agree to
8 propose  9 be willing to  10 provided
11 think we can accept  12 depends on  13 can offer

**7**  1 No, he hasn't – he can't see an easy solution.
2 It's not clear if Malcolm believes one side is right, but he says the student gives the impression she's telling the truth.

**8**  The seven verbs are: insists, admits, claims, is refusing, think(s), suspects, points out.
1 insists  2 points out  3 suspects

**9**  1 She admits that she **did find** information online.
2 **What struck me was** how distressed she seems.
3 **She does give** the impression that she's being honest.
4 **It was Kaitlin who brought** the dispute to my attention.
5 **Not only does he think** that its contents are plagiarised, **but he also suspects** it was written by somebody else.

## INTERVIEW Negotiation styles

**2**  1 Di  2 both  3 Andrés  4 Di

**3**  1 At a cable television channel in Guatemala.
2 He wanted to introduce planning in different areas.
3 They didn't like them and resisted them because they were used to doing things without planning them first.
4 He suggested that they only use planning for resources, vehicles and cameras.
5 They had to let him know where they were going, what they were doing, and what equipment they needed.
6 People started to be happier and work faster, and the flow of production worked more smoothly.
7 To use planning in other areas.

**4**  1 used  2 please  3 want  4 instead  5 let's  6 planning
7 letting  8 started

**5**  1 big  2 generally not  3 smaller groups  4 different  5 seem to agree

**6**  1 the act/task of getting things to be decided during a meeting
2 the act of making decisions / finding solutions after the meeting
3 the way of negotiating in Western culture
4 the way Western business people can see/interpret a meeting with Eastern business people
5 the fact that the meeting did not go as well as the Western business people had thought

## Unit 14

**1** 1 d 2 h 3 b 4 g 5 a 6 e 7 c 8 f

**2** a Predictions 1 and 8 b Predictions 3, 4 and 6

**3** 1 by 2030 2 in about 2040 3 in the future
4 in the long term / by the end of the century
5 before long / by the mid-2020s
6 by the mid-2020s / before long
7 by the end of the century / in the long term

**4** 1 will have left 2 will be living 3 'll/will be working
4 'll/will have had 5 'll/will be cohabiting 6 won't have got
7 'll/will be renting 8 will have bought

**5** Possible answers:
1 I might have moved to a new house by the end of next year.
2 I'll be sleeping at midnight tonight.
3 I hope to be working when I'm 65.
4 I won't have stopped driving for ecological reasons by 2030.
5 I might have taken up a new hobby by this time next year.
6 I should be studying English in five years' time.
7 I may have had a holiday in space by 2050.
8 I'd like to be running my own business in ten years from now.

**6** 1 reasons for 2 confident that 3 contributions; make
4 hope; achieved 5 How; handle 6 intend to 7 what; doing
8 would; say

**7** 1 candidate 2 covering letter 3 CV 4 experience
5 graduate 6 internship 7 interview stage
8 newly graduated 9 main objective 10 psychology
11 references 12 salary 13 sell yourself 14 style
15 submit

**9** Viral pandemic, Take-over by robots

**10** 1 high 2 8 3 5 4 very high

**11** a 2 b 4 c 1 d 3

**12** 1 4 2 2 3 1 4 3 5 2 6 4

**13** 1 worst case scenario 2 widespread 3 flashpoints
4 on a global scale 5 setback 6 obliterated
7 burst out / erupt

## DOCUMENTARY The Antarctic researcher

**1 & 2** 1 South Pole (this answer isn't in the video)
2 was 3 can 4 live 5 driest 6 no

**3** 1 Poland 2 cartography
3 geography data analyst (Magda says *analysis*, but this is a
grammatical error)
4 (cartographical) maps, satellite images and aerial photography
5 the terrain, temperature changes, changes to glaciers

**4** MAGIC = Mapping and Geographic Information Centre
GIS = geographic information system

**5** 1 It's the leading organisation doing research there (and
monitoring and making observations).
2 For more than sixty years.
3 In the (nineteen) eighties.
4 Glaciology, geology and biology.
5 One is a research ship, the other has a logistics role (bringing
food, equipment and clothing).
6 Skis. They allow the planes to land anywhere.

**6** 1 penguins / penguin colonies / penguin poo
2 where the colonies were
3 thirty-eight penguin colonies
4 there were some that nobody knew about
5 took high-resolution photos of the colonies
6 counting the penguins

**7** 1 In 2007
2 Two
3 To return to Antarctica in November and as many times as
possible.
4 Flying over glaciers and ice-shelves (and seeing the changes)
5 It's her dream job (= she loves it)

**8** a remote b wildlife c chick d unspoilt
e stain f resolution

# Critical incidents

**GRAMMAR**

Making deductions about the past

**1** Complete the conversation using the modal verbs in the box. Use each modal verb at least once.

| can't | could | couldn't | may | might | must |

**LI** I'm sorry I'm late. Is Ting here?

**MEI** No, she isn't, which is odd, because she's normally so punctual.

**LI** She ⁱ_____ well have got lost. This is a very hard street to find.

**MEI** But she's been here before, so she ²_____ have got lost. And anyway, she would have phoned if she'd got lost or delayed, so she ³_____ be on her way. I'm sure she'll be here any minute now.

**LI** She ⁴_____ have just forgotten about the meal. That's always a possibility.

**MEI** She ⁵_____ have forgotten. She phoned this afternoon to ask if she should bring anything.

**LI** Well, she ⁶_____ have got stuck in traffic. It can sometimes be busy at this time of the day.

**MEI** On a Sunday? I don't think so!

**LI** Have you checked your mobile? Maybe she's sent a message.

**MEI** Just a moment. Yes, there's a missed call from her. I didn't hear it, so she ⁷_____ have phoned when I was in the shower. I'll call her now.

**2** Read the situations and rewrite the <u>underlined</u> deductions with the correct modal verb + *have* + past participle.

## Mysteries from the past

### Mary Celeste, ghost ship

In December 1872, a ship was found in the Atlantic Ocean with no one on board. What had happened to its crew and passengers? ¹<u>Maybe they abandoned the ship in search of provisions.</u> However, there was plenty of food and water on board. One thing that stands out is that nothing of value was missing. ²<u>It's clear that it wasn't the result of a pirate attack.</u> ³<u>But it's very possible they left the ship through fear of an explosion.</u> Part of its cargo was 1,700 barrels of highly flammable alcohol. The lack of a clear explanation has led some people to another conclusion. ⁴<u>They are sure that the people on board were abducted by aliens.</u>

### The disappearance of the dinosaurs

Around 65 million years ago, the dinosaurs became extinct. Why did this happen? One thing is certain. ⁵<u>We're sure they didn't die out slowly.</u> There are plenty of dinosaur fossils from before 65 million years ago, and none after that. The impact of an asteroid is the most widely accepted explanation. If so, ⁶<u>there's no doubt that asteroid was enormous</u> – big enough to change the atmosphere around the planet. ⁷<u>There's a good chance an asteroid caused the dinosaurs to die out.</u> However, there are other possible explanations. ⁸<u>Perhaps they were wiped out by a massive volcanic eruption.</u> Climate change is also a possible explanation.

1 _____
_____

2 _____
_____

3 _____
_____

4 _____
_____

5 _____
_____

6 _____
_____

7 _____
_____

8 _____
_____

**8**

**VOCABULARY**
Describing
strong feelings

**3** Move one letter in each word to correct these expressions to describe strong feelings, and write them in pairs of expressions with a similar meaning.

> ascinafted   otu fo pacel   gintriued   rhorified   afflebd   thumiliaed
> trillehd   omrtified   ystimfied   aplpaled   eldighted   disolate

1 _____   _____        4 _____   _____
2 _____   _____        5 _____   _____
3 _____   _____        6 _____   _____

**4** Complete this description of working for a voluntary organisation in Togo in West Africa using the expressions from Exercise 3. Use each expression once. There may be more than one correct answer.

TOGO

Burkina
Faso

Benin

Nigeria

Ghana

Atlantic Ocean

**Over to you**

Describe a time when you experienced feelings expressed by words in Exercise 3.

# My volunteer experience in Togo

I'd been ¹_____ by anthropology for a long time, so one summer I applied to a local volunteer organisation to work on a project in Togo. They interviewed me, and I was ²_____ to be accepted.

The plane took us to Lomé, the capital city. I remember feeling ³_____ when I got my first sight of the city. However, once in the city I was ⁴_____ by the rubbish in the street and general lack of hygiene, with children washing themselves alongside animals.

We took a van to the village, about 50 kilometres away. I was ⁵_____ to see if it would be like the places I'd seen in documentaries and photos. The journey itself was scary. The van had at least twice the number of passengers it was designed for, and the headlights weren't working, so someone shone a torch on the road. I was ⁶_____ by the lack of attention to safety.

The village itself was a real culture shock. Many people had never met a European, so they stared and said things I didn't understand. Children wanted to touch my hair and babies cried in fear. I felt very ⁷_____ at first. But the people on the project made a big effort to make me feel at home, so I never felt ⁸_____ .

We all ate and lived together. The food was simple and repetitive, and there were things I didn't like, but my hosts would have been ⁹_____ if I'd turned down the little they had to offer, so I never let this show. Towards the end of my stay I was introduced to the head of the village. I knew I needed to be extremely respectful, and I was. Being the most important person in the local hierarchy, he would have felt ¹⁰_____ in front of his people if my behaviour had been at all casual or informal. It was an honour to meet him.

**VOCABULARY**
Reflecting on
the past

**5** Bela and Faisal are talking about their decision to live in another country. Complete their conversation using the words in the box. There may be more than one correct answer.

> a good thing   don't regret   glad   if only   not sorry   regret   sorry   wish

**FAISAL** My father's coming to see me.
**BELA** That's good.
**FAISAL** Yeah, but sometimes I ¹_____ coming to live in another country. On the one hand I'm ²_____ I came here because things have gone really well for me. But I ³_____ I hadn't come so far away. I've got kids and I'm ⁴_____ he hasn't seen them more often. What about you?
**BELA** I'm ⁵_____ I came to live here. My parents are just four hours away and I've got a lot of friends here, so I ⁶_____ my decision at all. Work's another matter. ⁷_____ I'd gone to university when I had the chance. I'm a bit fed up with working in cafés and restaurants.
**FAISAL** Right. I was thinking of dropping out of university at one point, but it's ⁸_____ I didn't. Being a qualified engineer has meant I've always been able to find jobs I like doing.

## GRAMMAR
Conditionals –
past and present

**6** Look at the sentences describing different events and situations. Use conditionals to rewrite each pair of sentences as a single sentence.

I didn't have anything to read. You lent me your newspaper.
If ¹ *I'd had something to read, you wouldn't have lent me your newspaper.* .
You lent me your newspaper. I saw that job ad.
If ² _____ .
I'm not working as a security guard. I applied for the job.
I ³ _____ .

James didn't ask her to marry him. She didn't say yes.
If ⁴ _____ .
They weren't married. She moved to Australia.
If ⁵ _____ .
She's living by a beach now. She didn't stay in the UK.
She ⁶ _____ .

## VOCABULARY
Disagreeing with
speculations

**7** Complete the way that B disagrees with A's speculations using *would / wouldn't have* and the correct form of the verbs in the box.

| find | hear | lie | see | take | tell |
|---|---|---|---|---|---|

1 **A** Fred must have won some money. He's buying a new house.
  **B** That can't be true. He _____ us about it.
2 **A** Gigi saw something in the sky last night. She thinks it could have been a UFO.
  **B** No way. Someone else _____ it too.
3 **A** Li said he didn't delete that photo, but he might not have been telling the truth.
  **B** He _____ about it. He's always very honest.
4 **A** The flat next door is empty. They must have moved out during the night.
  **B** No, we _____ them.
5 **A** Do you think the city of Atlantis might have existed?
  **B** No, they _____ it by now.
6 **A** Cindy must have borrowed the car. I can't find the keys anywhere.
  **B** But she _____ it without asking. Keep looking.

## VOCABULARY
Languages

**8** Complete the language words in this article about a multilingual family.

# A multilingual household

The language situation in our house is sometimes confusing, with four languages spoken. I'm from Scotland, so my ¹mo_____ to_____ is English. Hicham's from Morocco. Morocco's ²of_____ la_____ is Modern Standard Arabic, but Hicham's ³fi_____ la_____ is a ⁴di_____ of Standard Arabic called Moroccan Arabic. He also speaks good French as a ⁵se_____ la_____ . But we live in Spain, so Spanish is our ⁶co_____ la_____ . Hicham speaks a little English, but we never talk in English because he can't understand my Scottish ⁷ac_____ ! Our son speaks four languages, so he's ⁸mu_____ . That's because many people in Valencia are ⁹bi_____ and speak a ¹⁰re_____ la_____ called Valencian as well as Spanish.

## Over to you

What are the official languages where you live? What's your mother tongue? Do you speak any other languages?

# EXPLORE**Reading**

**9** Match the definitions (1–5) with the UK and US English words in the box.

behavior  behaviour  cell phone  mobile phone  favorite
favourite  pavement  sidewalk  subway  underground

| | | UK English | US English |
|---|---|---|---|
| 1 | a small object you use to communicate with people | | |
| 2 | the area next to a road where people walk | | |
| 3 | a railway that travels under a city | | |
| 4 | preferred, best-liked | | |
| 5 | a person's particular way of doing things | | |

**10** Make a list of typical complaints about mobile phones and their users.

**11** A woman in America has written to a newspaper to complain about mobile phone users. Read her complaints. Are they included on the list you made?

## Complaint Box | **Immobile on the phone**

*By PAMELA A. LEWIS*

1 This is a city of people who are constantly on the move. But lately I have noticed many who are completely immobile. Their favorite places to stand are on the subway stairs, either at the top, bottom or halfway up; at times, they camp in the middle of the sidewalk. Regardless of where these people choose to stop, they are all engaged in the same activity: talking on their cell phones. And while they chatter away, like statues newly bestowed with the gift of speech, the rest of us are obliged to perform something akin to interpretive dance to make our way around them.

2 I had a close encounter with this new brand of boor this summer. Before even reaching the entry to the station, I spotted her from a distance. As if glued to the top step and leaning against the steel railing, she was a textbook image of the cell phone user: oblivious to everything save the words she uttered and the ones coming from the stylish model she pressed firmly to her ear. As I neared the stairs, I felt my blood pressure inching up, yet I was determined to stay calm and noncombative.

3 'Excuse me, please,' I said, dredging up a courteousness I really didn't feel. No reaction. Once more into the breach: 'Excuse me, I need to get by,' I repeated, adding more

force to my tone. The statue turned her head, glowering at me. Mere seconds separated that indignant stare from my fate: Would I be tongue-lashed with a barrage of profanities? Hurled down the subway stairs I needed to descend? Or worse, would I be dispatched by the cell phone itself, swiftly transformed into a Bond-like instrument of death?

4 The statue moved slightly, just enough for me to make my way down; as the distance grew between us, I heard her grumble profanely something about 'these people asking me to move.'

5 I like the cell phone. There's one in my handbag, and on occasion I use it. It's practical and fun. But it has also changed our behavior, and not necessarily, I am discovering, for the better. Whether it's calling and texting while driving, or blocking the path of other pedestrians while conversing, the banging sound of civility's bar as it is lowered another notch is being heard more frequently.

6 It is always difficult to know at exactly what point such a shift occurs; when, say, the importance of one's call outruns everyone else's need to funnel down subway stairs or walk along the sidewalk. Yet its effects, however slight, can be felt.

7 We can call all we like; the least we can do is respectfully step aside while doing it.

**12** Choose the best summary of the woman's complaints.

a She thinks mobile phones are fun and she uses her mobile a lot. However, she always stands out of the way when she's talking, and she wishes other mobile phone users would do the same.

b She has nothing against mobile phones, and likes using them, but she doesn't like it when people on mobile phones block the way in the street or drive and use a mobile at the same time.

c She doesn't like people talking on mobile phones, although she has one and occasionally uses it. She thinks most mobile phone users are selfish, and don't consider the people around them.

**13** Choose the best way to complete these sentences.

1 The people the writer is complaining about are most often found _____.
a on underground stairs          b on the pavement

2 It's hard to pass by them because they _____.
a don't leave enough space          b move a lot, as if they were dancing

3 The woman on a mobile phone she describes was _____ example of the people she is complaining about.
a an unusual                              b a typical

4 When she spoke to the woman, she _____.
a felt very angry                        b made an effort to be polite

5 The woman's reaction to her second request was to _____ and then move.
a look angrily at her                  b shout at her

6 The writer thinks that people's bad behaviour when using mobile phones is

_____.

a  slowly getting better              b getting worse and worse

**14** The writer uses a number of images to bring her complaints to life. Find these words in the article and <u>underline</u> the expression they form part of. Which expression is used to describe 1–7 below?

| camp   interpretive dance   glued   breach   Bond-like   bar   funnel |

1 how immobile people on mobile phones are      *as if glued to the top step*

2 how standards of behaviour are falling          _____

3 how people stop in very inconvenient places   _____

4 how a lot of people go into a small space        _____

5 how asking to get by is like going into battle   _____

6 how difficult it can be to get past people        _____

7 how she imagines someone using their mobile

phone as a futuristic weapon from a film          _____

**15** What do you think these words and expressions from the text mean? Write a definition. Use the context to help you.

1 to chatter away (Paragraph 1)          _____

2 a boor (Paragraph 2)                        _____

3 inching up (Paragraph 2)                  _____

4 glowering (Paragraph 3)                    _____

5 tongue-lashed with a barrage of
profanities (Paragraph 3)                  _____

6 hurled (Paragraph 3)                        _____

7 to grumble (Paragraph 4)                  _____

**Over to you**

What do you think about the reader's complaint? Is the behaviour of mobile phone users a problem where you live?

## GLOSSARY

**bestow with** (verb): to give to someone
**akin to** (adjective): similar
**spot** (verb): to see or notice
**oblivious** (adjective): not conscious of what is happening around you
**courteousness** (noun): polite and respectful behaviour
**profanely** (adverb): in an offensive or obscene manner

**1** Before you watch, think about these questions.

Have you travelled to other countries? If so, what cultural differences did you notice? Can you recall any particular incidents involving these differences?

Aurora

Monica

**2** Watch the video and answer the questions about Aurora and Monica.

| | | Aurora | Monica |
|---|---|---|---|
| 1 | Where is she from? | _____ | _____ |
| 2 | Does she mention more than one cultural difference? | _____ | _____ |
| 3 | Does she mention a specific incident? | _____ | _____ |

**3** Watch Aurora again (0:11–1:00). Are the sentences true or false? Correct the false ones.

1 People where she comes from talk a lot but don't use their hands.  TRUE / FALSE
2 Photo a) shows a hug.  TRUE / FALSE
3 When travelling she never hugs people.  TRUE / FALSE
4 She thinks that people in other countries might not understand the significance of a hug.  TRUE / FALSE

**4** Choose the best definition of the underlined words in these extracts from what Aurora says. Watch again if necessary.

1 In the Caribbean, we talk a lot. We don't bother using our hands.
  a  make the effort to do something      b    feel comfortable
2 Whenever I'm out of my country I try not to do that.
  a  Sometimes when      b    Every or any time that
3 People might misinterpret our way of expression so I tone it down a little bit.
  a  exaggerate it      b    make it less energetic
4 They sometimes don't get what we're talking about.
  a  understand      b    like

**5** Watch Monica again (1:04–2:58) and answer the questions.

1 Where did the incident take place?
2 What did she do?
3 What was the other person's reaction? Why?
4 What did she notice on the menu? What did they mean?
5 How did she react to what she saw on the menu?
6 What's the situation for people in Spain with her eating habits?
7 What did the chef do? Why?

**6** There is an inconsistency in her anecdote. What is it? Watch again if necessary.

**7** Monica talks about what habitually happens in her country. Complete this extract with ways of talking about habitual behaviour. Watch again to check.

I'm vegetarian. In Spain that's not very ¹_____ at all and ²_____ you go to restaurants and then you ³_____ that there's nothing for you to eat even if it's just a one salad because it ⁴_____ tuna or something, and of course they ⁵_____ whether something is vegetarian or not.

**8** Is there a country with a very different culture that you would like to visit? What cultural differences would you expect to find there?

**GLOSSARY**

**tuna** (noun): a large fish which lives in warm seas; the flesh of this fish eaten as food

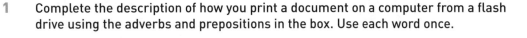

# How it's done

**GRAMMAR**

Verbs with adverbs and prepositions 1

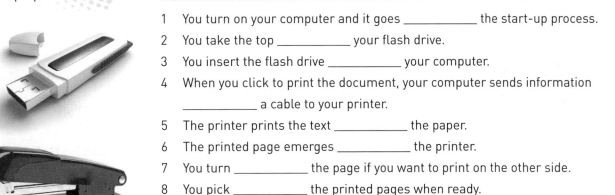

**1** Complete the description of how you print a document on a computer from a flash drive using the adverbs and prepositions in the box. Use each word once.

| along   from   into   off   onto   over   through   together   up |

1 You turn on your computer and it goes _____ the start-up process.
2 You take the top _____ your flash drive.
3 You insert the flash drive _____ your computer.
4 When you click to print the document, your computer sends information _____ a cable to your printer.
5 The printer prints the text _____ the paper.
6 The printed page emerges _____ the printer.
7 You turn _____ the page if you want to print on the other side.
8 You pick _____ the printed pages when ready.
9 You can use staples or a paper-clip to hold various sheets of paper _____ .

**2** Ⓒircle the correct options to complete this description of how a newspaper is made. Sometimes both options are possible.

---

◉◉◉
◀ ▶ ⟳ ⊠ + [                    ] ⌕Q⁻

### ⫸How a newspaper is made

The newspaper comes together in the newsroom. The reporters ¹put their stories onto / put onto their stories the computer system. The editorial team then chooses stories, adds advertising and editorial material, and ²puts the paper together / puts together the paper. They then read through the pages to correct any errors. The file now is ready to send to the printing press.

The file ³goes along a digital cable / goes a digital cable along to printing presses. Here, a supervisor ⁴turns into the file / turns the file into a film, and then ⁵exposes onto the film / exposes the film onto an aluminium plate with a plastic surface. A laser beam ⁶cuts the contents onto the plastic / cuts onto the contents the plastic. It's the plate that ⁷prints onto the newspaper / prints the newspaper onto its pages.

During printing, robots ensure a continuous supply of paper ⁸goes into the press / goes the press into. The newspaper ⁹emerges from the press / emerges the press from as continuous sheets of paper and machines ¹⁰cut into the sheets / cut the sheets into double pages and automatically ¹¹put together the pages / put the pages together to make the finished newspapers. Sometimes staples are added to ¹²hold the pages together / hold together the pages.

---

**VOCABULARY**

Organising a description

**3** Put the words in the correct order to make expressions for organising the description of a process.

a done / this / once / is _____
b told / you / I / remember / about / you _____
c first / the / is / thing _____
d process / and / the / that's / whole _____
e step / next / is / the _____
f minute / that / I'll / in / explain / a _____
g is / happens / next / what _____

**4** Match the expressions (a–g) in Exercise 3 with the gaps (1–7) in this talk about how chocolate is made. Write the letter in the gap. There may be more than one correct answer.

'So, how is our chocolate made? Here's a brief description. ¹_c_, cocoa pods are cut off the cocoa trees, and the beans are extracted, left to ferment and then dried. Exactly how they're dried is important, but ²___. ³___, the beans are brought to the factory, where they are roasted. ⁴___, they're broken into small pieces and ground between rollers to make a liquid called cocoa liquor. This contains cocoa and cocoa butter, and some of the cocoa butter is pressed out. ⁵___, the liquid is left to cool down and solidify and is ground to make cocoa powder. This is then mixed with a variety of ingredients – mainly cocoa butter and sugar – to produce chocolate. ⁶___ the importance of the drying process: the beans can be dried artificially, but the flavour is better if they are dried in the sun. We dry our beans in the sun for seven days or more to give the best possible taste. ⁷___. Has anybody got any questions?'

**5** Complete the words in these expressions using vowels. In which gaps (1–7) could you put them in the description in Exercise 4?

1  F_ll_w_ng th_t   _____
2  F_rst _f _ll   _____
3  _ _rl__r l
   m_nt__ _n_d   _____
4  T_ st_rt _ff   _____

5  _ft_r th_t   _____
6  _nd th_t's _t   _____
7  T_ b_g_n w_th   _____
8  I'll c_m_ b_ck t_
   th_t l_t_r   _____

**Over to you**

Can you describe how any other products are made?

**VOCABULARY**

Describing responsibilities

**6** Complete the three job adverts using the words in the box. There may be more than one correct answer.

accountable  answer  charge  duties  manage  oversee
report  responsibility  responsible  supervising  task  up

**The Huntington Telegraph** is looking for a Chief Editor and Sub-Editor. The Chief Editor's ¹_____ include making the final decision about contents, and ²_____ the team in the press room. Sub-editors ³_____ to the editors and their main ⁴_____ is to check that news stories are well written. It is also their ⁵_____ to add headlines.

**The Learn Fast Institute** is an international chain of language schools that is expanding rapidly. We are currently seeking someone to ⁶_____ our London office. The successful candidate will ⁷_____ the day-to-day running of the office, and will be directly ⁸_____ to the school's Director.

**Adventure Now** would like to employ a Team Leader to work at our Melbourne-based Executive Adventure Centre. Team leaders are in ⁹_____ of organising team-building activities at the centre and it's ¹⁰_____ to them to ensure all members participate as fully as possible in the challenges that the team is set. Team leaders ¹¹_____ to our Project Manager, who is ¹²_____ for designing activity programmes.

**Over to you**

Which of these jobs would you most like to do? Why? Write an advert for your own job or another job.

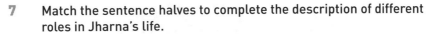

Describing roles

**7** Match the sentence halves to complete the description of different roles in Jharna's life.

*Jharna*

1  I work ...
2  I've taken ...
3  I do voluntary ...
4  I act ...
5  I play an ...
6  I belong ...
7  I'm a ...
8  I'm a member ...

a  work for a nursing home for the elderly.
b  of a sports centre near my house.
c  supporter of my local cricket team.
d  as a nurse in a hospital.
e  on the role of union representative at work.
f  to a local political group that promotes green policies.
g  active part in decision-making at my child's school.
h  as secretary at meetings at the nursing home.

Organising a talk

**8** Complete the expressions in these extracts from a talk about traditional Irish music.

Good evening, and thanks for coming to the concert. Before we start, I'm going to talk a little about the music we play and **¹**I'll b_____ lo_____ at three m_____ a_____ – the music, its history and how we play it.

**²**Le_____ b_____ with the music. We play traditional Irish music, and the vast majority of the tunes in our repertoire are dance tunes. That means ...

... **³**That's a_____ I w_____ to s_____ about the music for now. **⁴**N_____, I'd l_____ t_____ s_____ so_____ about its history. Now, some of the tunes played in Irish music were written by known composers, but most of the repertoire we play ...

... **⁵**That's i_____ as f_____ a_____ the history is co_____. **⁶**L_____ mo_____ o_____ to how we play the music. We're what's known as a ceilidh band, which means ...

... **⁷**O_____, t_____ how we play the music. At this point I think it's best for me to stop talking and we'll play our first set of tunes. Please feel free to dance!

**9** Rewrite the ways of organising a talk using the words in brackets and three other words or contractions.

**Outlining the structure of a talk**

1  like / talk / three main things

_____

2  divided / talk / three parts

_____

**Opening a topic**

3  next / is / history

_____

4  now / take / look / its history

_____

**Closing a topic**

5  so / talked / we play the music

_____

# EXPLORE**Writing**

**10** Imagine someone is going to substitute you for a few weeks at work or in another position of responsibility. Make a note of your answers to these questions from your substitute.

1 What's your job or position? You can invent one if necessary.
2 What are your working hours?
3 What are your responsibilities?
4 What needs to be done immediately?
5 What jobs or tasks need to be dealt with after that?
6 Are there any computer passwords that I need to know?
7 Who can I contact if I need help, and how do I contact them?

**11** Read the handover note that Tanya has left for her substitute. Does it answer the questions in Exercise 10? If so, does it give a complete answer?

---

### Handover note for the post of volunteer co-ordinator

Dear Melissa

My maternity leave has started earlier than expected, so unfortunately I won't be able to talk you through the job. However, I hope these notes will allow you to hit the ground running.

This is a part-time voluntary post and should only <u>take you</u> two evenings a week. The main duties <u>include</u> contacting volunteers, preferably by phone, to make sure that there are enough people to run events, and being present at least one event a week to oversee volunteers and stand in for anyone who fails to turn up. Typically, volunteers are needed to sell tickets on the door, show people to their seats, work behind the bar and help behind the scenes. <u>You'll find</u> a list of volunteers and their contact details on the office computer, and the centre manager creates a document for each event <u>detailing</u> the number and type of volunteers needed. I've found volunteers for the show on Saturday night, so your first job will be to cover the jazz on Sunday lunchtime.

That's all I can think of for now. If you have any <u>doubts</u>, contact Jo, the office manager. She's in the office every morning from 9 till 1 and three afternoons a week. In an emergency, <u>don't hesitate</u> to phone me, though there's no guarantee I'll be able to answer.

Good luck!

Tanya

---

**12** Which of the <u>underlined</u> words and expressions in the handover note could be substituted by 1–6 below?

1 listing _____   4 occupy _____
2 please feel free _____   5 there's _____
3 involve _____   6 questions _____

**13** Write a handover note for the job or position you answered the questions about in Exercise 10. Include some of the expressions from Exercise 12 and any other useful expressions from Tanya's handover note.

## Before you watch

1  What is the difference between these words? Use the glossary to check your answers.

    1  *lecturer* and *professor*
    2  *lawyer*, *barrister* and *judge*
    3  *refugee* and *asylum*

2  You are going to watch a video of a lawyer, Guglielmo, talking about his work and its connection with the United Nations. Can you complete this overview of the United Nations?

Guglielmo

The United Nations (UN) is an international organisation that was founded in 1945 after the Second World War. Its aim is to maintain international peace and security, develop friendly relations among nations and promote social progress, better living standards and human rights.

The UN's main bodies include:

- The ¹Gen_____ Ass_____ , where all members have equal power. ☐
- The ²Sec_____ Cou_____ , responsible for maintaining peace between countries. ☐
- The International ³Cou_____ of Jus_____ , the UN's main judicial organ ☐

The UN also runs a number of specialised programmes, which include:

- The ⁴Chi_____'s Fund (UNICEF), which protects the rights of young people. ☐
- The High Commission for Refugees (UNHCR), which protects refugees' rights. ☐
- The ⁵Dev_____ Programme (UNDP), which helps people to build a better life. ☐

## While you watch

3  Watch the complete video. Check your answers to Exercise 2 and put the UN bodies and programmes in the order in which Guglielmo mentions them.

4  Watch Part 1 again (0:09–1:40) and complete the sentences.

    1  Guglielmo works as _____ .
    2  His field of interest is _____ .
    3  His interest comes from a teacher who was the first _____ .
    4  The main institution that deals with international law is _____ .
    5  Membership of this institution now includes _____ .

**5** Watch Part 2 again (1:35–2:40) and answer the questions.

1 What decision led to Guglielmo's stay in Africa?
2 What type of work did he do there?
3 What were the particular aims of this work?
4 Where exactly did he do his work?

**6** Guglielmo says that he became particularly interested in questions of accountability. From the context, what do you think accountability means? Choose the best answer.

a how organisations with power take responsibility for their actions
b how organisations with power finance their actions
c how organisations with power make decisions

**7** Watch Part 3 again (2:43–4:39) and circle the correct option to complete the sentences.

1 He thought the 9/11 terrorist attacks in New York in 2001 might make the UN stronger / weaker.
2 That's because when a country's national security is threatened, it is more / less likely to use international institutions.
3 Since the 9/11 attacks he thinks there has generally been a lot of / little consensus between nations.
4 He would like to see an improvement in the UN's accountability / use of sanctions and force.

# After you watch

**8** Match the halves of these extracts from what Guglielmo says.

1 Public International Law [...] is the law that governs ... ☐
2 The UN created [...] a programme that focuses ... ☐
3 I took the decision to explore ... ☐
4 I decided to undertake ... ☐
5 I investigated [...] the extent to which refugees enjoyed ... ☐
6 Its main function there was to provide ... ☐
7 When an organisation exercises ... ☐

a their fundamental human rights.
b the field in a more practical sense.
c relations between states.
d humanitarian assistance.
e more powers, the issue of accountability will become more and more central.
f on development – the UNDP.
g research in Africa.

**9** Would you like to do the jobs that Guglielmo does or has done? Why? / Why not?

---

### GLOSSARY

**barrister** (noun): a type of lawyer in Britain, Australia and some other countries who is qualified to give specialist legal advice and can argue a case in both higher and lower law courts, as opposed to a *solicitor*, who is trained to prepare cases and give advice on legal subjects and can represent people in lower courts

**professor** (noun): a teacher of the highest rank in a department of a British university

**judge** (noun): a person who is in charge of a trial in a court and decides how a person who is guilty of a crime should be punished

**refugee** (noun): a person who has escaped from their own country for political, religious or economic reasons or because of a war

**asylum** (noun): protection or safety, especially that given by a government to foreigners who have been forced to leave their own countries for political reasons

**accountable** (adjective): someone who is accountable is completely responsible for what they do and must be able to give a satisfactory reason for it

**at stake** (expression): in a situation where something might be lost

**range (from ... to)** (verb): to have an upper and a lower limit in amount, number, etc.

# 10 Discovery

**VOCABULARY**
Exploration and discovery

**1** Complete the words in these stories of discoveries.

## SIGNS OF LIFE

In 2004, the remains of tiny ancient people were [1]di_____ on Flores Island in Indonesia. Because of their size, they were nicknamed 'Hobbits'. A few years later, more similar-sized bones were [2]lo_____ on the South Pacific islands of Palau. This led to an intense debate. Were they small humans, or were they a distinct species? And when modern humans [3]re_____ Flores Island about 12,000 years ago, did they meet the Hobbits? Flores Island legends suggest they might have done.

From 1963 to 1998, the Big Ear telescope in Ohio, USA, [4]sc_____ the skies to [5]se_____ f_____ signs of alien life. In 1977, Dr Jerry Ehman [6]de_____ a strong radio signal while working on the telescope. It was so strong that he wrote 'Wow!' on the computer print-out. Was it an attempt by an alien life form to communicate with us?

People [7]d_____ re_____ i_____ global warming have long used satellite images to [8]m_____ environmental changes around the world. But images from Google Earth are allowing everybody to [9]ex_____ the planet. By studying images of the Amazon basin, researchers in Brazil recently [10]f_____ ev_____ o_____ an ancient civilisation that has been revealed by deforestation. It was generally thought that there were no complex civilisations here before Europeans invaded.

**VOCABULARY**
Describing benefits

**2** Complete the sentences about the benefits of different things by adding one or two words from the box to each gap if necessary. Some gaps do not need any words.

> are  for  is  of  on  to  us  would

1 Space missions enable _____ develop new technology.

2 If we all became vegetarian, it _____ have a positive effect _____ our environment.

3 Finally understanding our universe _____ benefit _____ us all.

4 Genetic research _____ crucial _____ discovering the cure for illnesses.

5 Nuclear power stations give _____ the ability _____ produce energy without pollution.

6 Reducing carbon emissions _____ improve _____ lives around the world.

7 Internet access _____ essential _____ following world events.

8 Cheap solar energy _____ be _____ considerable benefit _____ people in developing countries.

9 Genetically modified crops will allow _____ grow food in difficult places.

10 Research on animals _____ vital _____ making safe medicines.

**Over to you**

Do you agree with the sentences in Exercise 2? If not, explain why.

**3**  (Circle) the correct verb forms.

1   When do you think / thinking more clearly – after get / getting up, or before go / going to bed?
2   Do you spend / spending a lot of time do / doing housework?
3   When you have a lot of things to do / doing, does it help you to make / making a list?
4   Are you interested / interesting in learn / learning another language or skill? If so, which one?
5   What would you do / doing if you were offered a good job, but had to work / working in another country?
6   Did you use to make / making study / studying a priority when you were a teenager?
7   Is climate change cause / causing a lot of controversy because it's hard to understand / understanding the science behind it?
8   Put / Putting an end to poverty is often a government's priority, but do politicians really have the will to succeed / succeeding?
9   Which is the most challenged / challenging issue faced / facing your country?

**4**  **Read Jeff's email to Davinda about his plans for the future. Find and correct eight words that should be *-ing* forms.**

Hi Davinda

I think I've decided what I'm going to do after I finish studying. I'm plan to spend a year travel around Europe. But I also want to do something that doesn't only involve visit nice places. I've been do some research on the Internet and I think voluntary work would be an interest thing to do. For example, there are lots of organic farms where you can work in exchange for food and accommodation. I wouldn't want to spend so much time away from home without bring something back with me, so after gain some experience, maybe organic farm is an area I could work in back home. What do you think? Maybe we could work on the same farm for a while.

Jeff

**5**  **Match the sentence halves to complete the descriptions of two famous people. Can you name them? Look in the box on the left to see who they are.**

1   This Polish-born scientist was a top ...
2   She worked with her husband, Pierre, ...
3   Her greatest accomplishments ...
4   She won international acclaim ...
5   After her husband's death, she dedicated ...

a   include the discovery of polonium and radium.
b   expert on radioactivity.
c   and awards, including two Nobel Prizes.
d   herself to teaching and investigating radium.
e   to investigate the properties of radioactive elements.

**Who was she?** _____

6   This Indian lawyer made ...
7   He used his knowledge and position to ...
8   He showed people ...
9   His successful non-violent protests changed ...
10  He faced some very tough ...

f   benefit less fortunate people in his country.
g   people's minds and behaviour.
h   challenges in his fight for Indian independence.
i   the defence of civil rights his life's work.
j   that you can use non-violent means to achieve your objectives.

**Who was he?** _____

The woman is Marie Curie. The man is Mohandas 'Mahatma' Gandhi.

## VOCABULARY
Giving and comparing sources

**6** Read the biography of the blues musician Robert Johnson and rewrite the <u>underlined</u> phrases using the words in the box.

| according | agreement | claim | differ | mention | who / ask |

1  *Sources differ on when* _____
2  _____
3  _____
4  _____
5  _____
6  _____

For such an influential artist, very little is known about travelling blues musician Robert Johnson. ¹<u>Sources vary about when</u> he was born. ²<u>Depending on where you look</u>, he was born in either 1911 or 1912, but probably on May 8. Much of what we know about him comes from interviews with musicians who had met him. ³<u>In Son House's version</u> of events, Johnson followed him around and wanted to copy his guitar playing when he first met him, but when he met him again a few months later, he had made miraculous progress. This led to the legend that Johnson had been taught to play by the devil at a crossroads one night. ⁴<u>In other sources it states that</u> his progress was the result of a year of practice with guitarist Ike Zimmerman. His death is equally mysterious. It is often repeated that he died of poisoning, though ⁵<u>his death certificate says nothing about this</u> as the cause of death. One thing is clear, though. ⁶<u>All sources agree that</u> in his brief life, during which he only made a small number of recordings, his outstanding playing, singing and song writing made him one of the all-time greats.

## VOCABULARY
Rights and obligations

**7** Complete the sentences about rights and obligations in the UK using the words in the box and *to* or *of*. There may be more than one correct answer.

| compulsory | duty | expected | free | freedom | obliged | option | right |

**Rights**
1  Students are _____ _____ choose which university they study at, providing their marks are good enough.
2  People have the _____ _____ organise peaceful protests in public.
3  Working fathers have the _____ _____ taking up to two weeks of paid leave when their child is born.
4  You have the _____ _____ leave home without carrying any form of identification.

**Obligations**
5  You are _____ _____ buy a licence for your television.
6  It's _____ for all passengers in a car _____ wear a seatbelt.
7  On public transport, younger people are _____ _____ give up their seat to an elderly person.
8  It's your _____ _____ be a member of a jury at a trial if you are called up.

### Over to you
**Compare the rights and obligations in the UK with those in your country.**

# EXPLORE**Reading**

**8** Match the words connected to space exploration (1–5) with the definitions (a–e).

| | | | |
|---|---|---|---|
| 1 | cosmos | a | a vehicle that can travel in space |
| 2 | spacecraft | b | a US government organisation responsible for space exploration |
| 3 | NASA | c | the distance that light travels in a year, used to measure distances in space |
| 4 | solar system | | |
| 5 | light year | d | the whole universe |
| | | e | a star and the planets that orbit it |

**9** Read the title of the article opposite. What do you think the sentence in brackets means? Read the first paragraph and then choose the best definition of 'a catch'.

A 'catch' is ...
a a hidden problem in a situation that is otherwise very good.
b the thing that makes a situation very good.

**10** Before you read the rest of the article, decide which *two* of these statements you think are *not* true. Then read and check your answers.

1 Astronauts are predicted to reach Mars by 2050.
2 The journey to Mars would take less than a year.
3 NASA has a duty to bring its astronauts back home.
4 In the future, space exploration may be carried out by commercial companies.
5 These days, space exploration is done for power.
6 A return trip to the nearest star to our solar system is feasible with today's technology.

**11** Answer these questions in your own words.

1 According to John Olson, how popular would a one-way journey into space be?

_____

2 What comparison does he use to justify his opinion?

_____

3 Why does he think we'll return to the moon?

_____

4 What does Robert Park mean when he talks about 'manned space flight'?

_____

5 What problem does he see with very long space missions?

_____

6 What alternative does he suggest?

_____

**Over to you**

What do you think about very long manned space missions? Would the financial investment be justified? Would you be interested in volunteering for one? Do you think it's wrong for a child to be born in space?

**12** Circle the correct definition for these words and phrases from the article.

1 cooped up (Paragraph 2)
  a moving fast
  b kept in a closed place
2 deter (Paragraph 2)
  a stop
  b encourage
3 set their sights on (Paragraph 3)
  a observe
  b decide to visit

4 shed (Paragraph 4)
  a remove, get rid of
  b respect
5 foreseeable (Paragraph 5)
  a that exists now
  b that you can predict or imagine
6 doom (sb) to (Paragraph 6)
  a give (sb) the opportunity to
  b force (sb) to do something unpleasant

# Space exploration volunteers wanted (The catch? It's a one-way ticket)

**1** It is often described as 'the final frontier'. The phrase, though, may take an even more literal meaning for those exploring space in the future. The next generation of astronauts may hurtle through the cosmos for years or decades on a mission to explore distant planets and stars – and never return.

**2** The prospect of spending years cooped up in a spacecraft would not deter people from applying, a senior NASA official has said. 'You would find no shortage of volunteers,' said John Olson, NASA's director of exploration systems integration. 'It's really no different from the pioneering spirit of many in past history, who took the one-way trip across the ocean with no intention of ever returning.'

**3** If, as Olson predicts, humans reach Mars by the middle of this century, engineers and astronauts may then set their sights on the frozen planets, fiery moons and stars beyond. 'We're going back to the moon, not for flags and footsteps but for a sustained presence,' Olson said. 'We're going to use the moon as a stepping stone to Mars and we're going to look at all the other exciting places to go in this solar system.'

**4** NASA is currently bound by President John F Kennedy's directive to bring its astronauts home. But the other nations rapidly developing space programmes may shed the constraint, as could the commercial companies that may supplant national efforts. 'Space is no longer for power and prestige; it's truly for economic benefit,' the Apollo 11 flight director Eugene Kranz said.

**5** With currently foreseeable technology, a round trip to Mars would take two to three years – a journey of six to nine months each way and a year-long mission on the surface. The star nearest Earth's solar system, Alpha Centauri, is 4.37 light years away, or more than 2.5 trillion miles.

**6** Robert Park, a physicist and prominent critic of manned space flight, said that even a one-way trip to Alpha Centauri was beyond the laws of physics. The energy

required to push a spacecraft up to the speed needed to get to the star within 50 years was so great as to be barely conceivable. 'A multigenerational space ark would doom the children raised to continue the mission never to see Earth and would decide their destiny before their birth, raising profound ethical questions.'

**7** Rather than devote immeasurable resources to sending humans into space, Park said science should instead build stronger telescopes to better study distant stars and planets.

## GLOSSARY

**hurtle** (verb): to move very fast
**prospect** (noun): the idea of something that will or might happen in the future
**pioneering** (adjective): using ideas and methods that have never been used before
**bound** (adjective): having a moral or legal duty to do something
**constraint** (noun): something which controls what you do by keeping you within particular limits
**supplant** (verb): to replace

**1** **Before you watch, think about this question. Then make notes under the headings below.**

What changes have there been over recent years in the place where you come from?

Cities and city life: _____

Transport: _____

Energy use and production: _____

Recycling and the environment: _____

**2** **Watch the video and tick (✓) any things in your notes that Liu or Adriana mention.**

**3** **Watch Liu again (0:11–1:09) and answer the questions.**

1 How often has she returned to China over the last nine years?
2 Where has she seen changes?
3 What are the first changes that she mentions?
4 What does she say is good about some changes?
5 What example does she give of a negative change?
6 How old were the trees that she talks about?

Liu       Adriana

**4** **Complete the ways that Liu talks about changes. Watch again to check.**

1 I've just realised _____ big the changes (are).

2 I see buildings _____ higher and more cars _____ than bicycles.

3 I _____ _____ ride my bike to go to school every day.

4 The road was _____ because there're more cars so they need to build a wider road.

5 I feel really sad, like those trees are part of my childhood memory but now they're just _____

_____ .

**5** **Watch Adriana again (1:12–2:02) and ⟨circle⟩ the correct options.**

1 Adriana is working / doing a postgraduate course at the moment.
2 Her area of expertise is how to get rid of / reduce waste.
3 The amount of waste produced by a process depends / doesn't depend on the amount of resources used.
4 New technologies mean you can have a bigger / smaller reactor.
5 This type of reactor will use more / less* materials and produce more / less waste.
6 Using less energy is normally / always good for the environment.

**6** **Watch Liu and Adriana again. How do they pronounce s in the underlined words? ⟨Circle⟩ the correct sound.**

1 I used to ride my bike to go to school every day.    /z/    /s/    /ʒ/
2 Minimise the resources that are used.                 /z/    /s/    /ʒ/
3 You usually have a big reactor.                        /z/    /s/    /ʒ/
4 You could use less* materials.                         /z/    /s/    /ʒ/

\* The use of *less* with a plural countable noun is a common error in English. The correct word here would be *fewer*.

---

**GLOSSARY**

**PhD** (noun): abbreviation for Doctor of Philosophy: the highest college or university degree
**waste** (noun): unwanted matter or material of any type
**reactor** (noun): a large machine in which atoms are either divided or joined in order to produce power

# Questions, questions

VOCABULARY
Expressions with people

**Over to you**

Can you think of another person or situation that helps to illustrate the meaning of each of the expressions?

VOCABULARY
Interviewing

**1** Complete the words in these sentences.

1 Sports coaches are responsible for motivating players. Their job is to g_ _ t_ _ _ b_ _ _ _ o_ _ o_ people.

2 Asking somebody about their job is a good way to break the ice. The subject of work usually g_ _ _ people t_ _ _ _ _ _ _.

3 Conmen are people who trick others into giving them money. They know how to m_ _ _ _ _ _ _ _ _ _ people.

4 People often stop talking when they are asked to reveal personal or secret information. They c_ _ _ _ u_.

5 School teachers sometimes deal with difficult students and parents. They need to be able to h_ _ _ _ _ people well.

6 Having to queue for a long time makes many people tense. It p_ _ _ people o_ e_ _ _.

7 People are more receptive to comedy if they feel relaxed, so comedians quickly aim to p_ _ their audience a_ e_ _ _.

8 Driving makes some people behave aggressively. It b_ _ _ _ _ _ o_ _ t_ _ w_ _ _ _ i_ them.

**2** Match each gap in the radio interview below with three of these expressions. Write the letters of the correct expressions in each gap.

| | | | |
|---|---|---|---|
| a | What do you mean? | g | You said something about being … |
| b | Is that right? | h | Have I got that right? |
| c | Tell me more about that. | i | So, … |
| d | You seem to be saying that … | j | In what sense? |
| e | Am I right? | k | Basically, … |
| f | You say you were … | l | You mentioned being … |

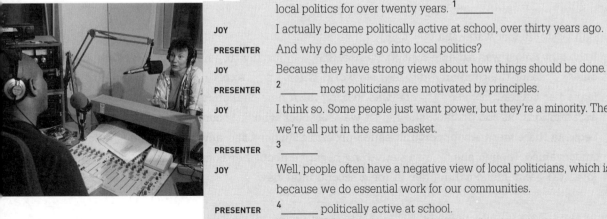

**PRESENTER** My first guest today is local politician Joy Davies. Joy, you've been involved in local politics for over twenty years. ¹_____

**JOY** I actually became politically active at school, over thirty years ago.

**PRESENTER** And why do people go into local politics?

**JOY** Because they have strong views about how things should be done.

**PRESENTER** ²_____ most politicians are motivated by principles.

**JOY** I think so. Some people just want power, but they're a minority. The problem is, we're all put in the same basket.

**PRESENTER** ³_____

**JOY** Well, people often have a negative view of local politicians, which is a shame because we do essential work for our communities.

**PRESENTER** ⁴_____ politically active at school.

**JOY** That's right. I joined a campaign to save the civic centre where I had ballroom-dancing classes. And we saved it!

**PRESENTER** Joy, thanks for coming on the show.

**JOY** You're welcome.

**3** Read these extracts from a difficult interview. Circle who said each thing – the interviewer (I) or the candidate (C). Then complete the reporting sentences using the verbs in the box. Use each verb once.

> admitted   advised   announced   apologised   challenged
> complained   promised   refused   thanked   threatened

1 'I'm sorry for arriving so late.'                                           I /(C)

   I _____*apologised*_____ for arriving so late.

2 'I'll send you my CV tomorrow.'                                           I / C

   I _____ to send him my CV tomorrow.

3 'To be honest, we're ideally looking for someone with more experience.'   I / C

   I _____ we were ideally looking for someone with
   more experience.

4 'Big companies never employ people from the north!'                       I / C

   I _____ that big companies never employed people
   from the north.

5 'Can you prove that's true about this company?'                           I / C

   I _____ him to prove that was true about this company.

6 'I'm going to stop the interview if you don't stop shouting.'             I / C

   I _____ to stop the interview if he didn't stop shouting.

7 'I won't answer any questions about my last job.'                         I / C

   I _____ to answer any questions about my last job.

8 'I'm leaving now, unless you have any other questions.'                   I / C

   I _____ that I was leaving unless he had any more
   questions.

9 'You should try to be more positive at your next interview.'             I / C

   I _____ him to be more positive at his next interview.

10 'Thank you for the advice, but I don't need it.'                          I / C

   I _____ him for the advice but told him I didn't need it.

**4** Circle the correct answers (a–c) to complete this report on a job interview. If two answers are possible, circle them both.

Candidate: Shiori Watanabe

I thought Shiori was an excellent candidate. She [1]___ for inviting her to an interview and she [2]___ about the company and how we work. When I [3]___ explain why she wanted to leave her current job, she [4]___ she was looking for a new challenge, which shows that she's an ambitious person. In fact, she [5]___ it was her boss who [6]___ consider changing jobs because there were few opportunities for promotion where she now works. She [7]___ feeling undervalued, though she [8]___ say anything negative about her company, which is a sign of loyalty. I recommend calling her in for a second interview.

| | | | |
|---|---|---|---|
| 1 | a thanked | b thanked me | c thanked to me |
| 2 | a asked | b asked me | c asked to me |
| 3 | a asked | b asked to | c asked her to |
| 4 | a said | b said me | c told me |
| 5 | a admitted | b admitted that | c admitted to |
| 6 | a advised | b advised her to | c advised to her |
| 7 | a admitted | b admitted to | c admitted that |
| 8 | a refused | b refused to | c refused me to |

**5** Complete the <u>underlined</u> part of each sentence using the correct form of the verbs. Add *to*, *for* and/or a pronoun if necessary. There may be more than one correct answer.

1  When I first met Katrina, <u>she / challenge / a game of chess</u>.

_____

2  <u>I / tell / I / not play well</u> and <u>she / promise / not play / her best</u>.

_____

3  I got angry recently when <u>a friend admit / lose a book I / lend him</u>.

_____

4  Later, <u>I / apologise / my angry reaction</u>.

_____

5  At the weekend, <u>my sister / announce / she / get married</u>.

_____

6  She knows I'm into photography, so she's <u>ask / take / photos at the wedding</u>.

_____

7  A police officer stopped me recently and <u>ask / see / my identification</u>.

_____

8  <u>He / threaten / arrest me</u> if I didn't have any identification on me.

_____

VOCABULARY
Giving statistics

**6** Decide which sentence (a–d) describes each phrase (1–6).

1  nearly 100 people ___

2  exactly 100 people ___

3  almost 100 people ___

4  just over 100 people ___

5  about 100 people ___

6  just under 100 people ___

a  We interviewed 100 people.
b  We interviewed 102 people.
c  We interviewed somewhere between 95 and 105 people.
d  We interviewed 97 people.

**7** Read the results of a survey and complete the phrases (1–10) using the words in the box.

> all   almost none   a fifth   just over half   most   nearly all
> none   four out of ten   just under a quarter   about a third

**Aim of survey:** To determine the lunchtime eating habits of city-centre workers
**Size of survey:** 100 people

**Results**

| | | |
|---|---|---|
| Have lunch between 12 and 2: | 100 | = [1]_____*All*_____ of the people |
| Usually buy takeaway food: | 83 | = [2]_____ of the people |
| Eat sandwiches: | 51 | = [3]_____ of the people |
| Sometimes take a packed lunch: | 24 | = [4]_____ of the people |
| Go home for lunch: | 0 | = [5]_____ of the people |
| Eat in a work canteen: | 6 | = [6]_____ of the people |
| Eat with colleagues: | 96 | = [7]_____ of the people |
| Eat fruit with lunch: | 40 | = [8]_____ of the people |
| Sometimes go to a restaurant: | 33 | = [9]_____ of the people |
| Eat in a local park: | 20 | = [10]_____ of the people |

**Over to you**

Write some sentences about typical lunchtime eating habits for people who work or study where you live.

# EXPLORE**Writing**

**8** A news researcher for a local radio station has written a report on the results of a recent opinion poll. Read the report and complete the key in the bar chart below using the categories in the box.

> Conservatives   Greens   Liberals   Socialists   Undecided

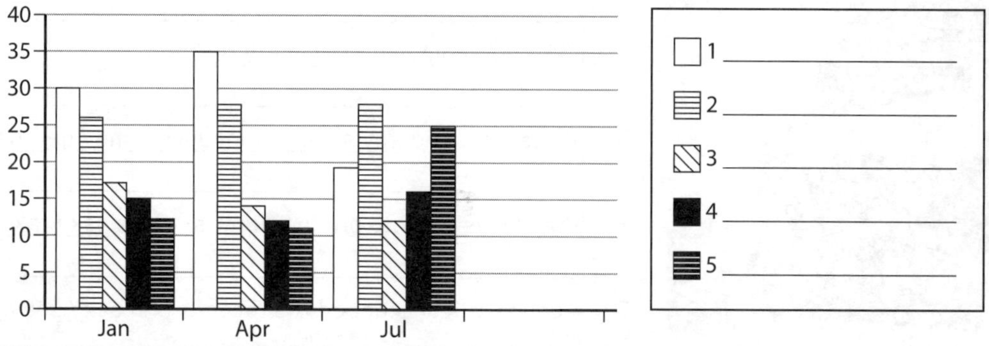

□ 1 _____
▤ 2 _____
▨ 3 _____
■ 4 _____
▤ 5 _____

### The July opinion poll and what it tells us

The chart shows the results (in percentages) of the latest opinion poll for September's local elections alongside poll results for April and January.

Two things in particular stand out. First, the Conservatives are in front for the first time. This is almost certainly due to recent financial scandals involving the Socialists, whose popularity <u>peaked</u> at almost 35% in April, but has <u>fallen</u> <u>sharply</u> since then. Second, while the percentage of voters who favour the Conservatives has <u>remained stable</u> over the last six months, there has been a <u>dramatic</u> <u>rise</u> in the number of undecided voters. This suggests that although many Socialist voters have lost faith in their party, they are not being won over by the Conservatives' message.

As for the smaller parties, the Greens have perhaps picked up votes from disenchanted Socialist voters, though the figures don't reveal a clear <u>pattern</u>. There has been a <u>gradual</u> <u>decrease</u> in support for the Liberals, however, and they look unlikely to get a good result.

Overall, the conclusion would seem to be that while voters are currently punishing the Socialists, both the Socialists and the Conservatives have a chance of winning the elections. The key will be who can persuade the one in four undecided voters to support them.

**9** Complete the words in these phrases from the report that are used to draw conclusions from the statistical information.

1 This is almost ce_____ d_____ to recent financial scandals …

2 This su_____ that although many Socialist voters have …

3 … the Greens have pe_____ picked up votes from …

4 … the figures don't re_____ a clear pattern.

5 … they lo_____ un_____ to get a good result.

6 Overall, the conclusion wo_____ se_____ to be that …

**10** Look at the result of the final opinion poll before the elections. Write a report about voting intentions now. Describe how they have changed and suggest possible reasons why. Alternatively, write about voting intentions where you live. Use some of the <u>underlined</u> expressions in the report, and words and expressions from Exercise 9.

| | |
|---|---|
| Conservatives: | 39% |
| Socialists: | 24% |
| Liberals: | 15% |
| Greens: | 11% |
| Undecided: | 11% |

**1**   Before you watch, think about these questions. Then make a list of things you should and should not do when you are at or getting ready for a job interview.

Have you ever been to a job interview? Did it go well? Why? / Why not?

You should: _____

You shouldn't: _____

**2**   Watch the video. Do Raquel or Anna Laura mention any of the things on your list?

**3**   Watch Raquel again (0:11–1:12) and (circle) the best option to complete the sentences.

1   Raquel's anecdote relates to something she ...
   a did.   b said.
2   Her mother lives ...
   a in the same city.
   b in another part of the country.
3   She went to the interview with her mother because ...
   a she was afraid.
   b they had to do something together afterwards.
4   The people interviewing her didn't ... the fact that she came with her mother.
   a like   b mind
5   She ... invited to a second interview.
   a was   b wasn't

Raquel

Anna Laura

**4**   Look at this extract from what Raquel says. Which of the words and phrases (a–e) below could you substitute for the examples of *like* (1–5)?

a   approve of   _____

b   erm   _____

c   for example   _____

d   similar to   _____

e   if / as though   _____

> I learnt that you shouldn't, er, bring your relatives to your interviews – it looks [1]**like** I was having a chaperone. Erm, they didn't [2]**like** it a lot at all, [3]**like** they asked me what is your mother doing here, I had to explain, [4]**like** er erm, we have to go somewhere else and she doesn't know the city so that's why I, I brought her er, it's not that, er, er, I need some company because I'm afraid of you or something [5]**like** that.

**5**   Watch Anna Laura again (1:16–2:47) and answer the questions.

1   What does Anna Laura do?
2   What surprises her about the people she interviews?
3   What did the first job she mentions involve doing?
4   Anna Laura mentions the need for *empathy* in this job. What is empathy?
5   Why didn't the man get the job?
6   What did the second job she mentions involve doing?
7   Why didn't the woman get the job?

**6**   Multi-word verbs are a common feature of spoken English. Match the multi-word verbs that Anna Laura uses with the definitions. Watch again if necessary to hear the verbs in context.

1   come along   a   to arrive or appear somewhere
2   come across   b   to become available
3   turn up   c   to meet and get on well with other people
4   mix with   d   to share the work that needs to be done
5   muck in   e   to give people the impression that you have a particular characteristic

**7**   Think about your job, or about a job you would like to do. What profile does a person need to do the job? Think of six questions you would ask someone at an interview for the job.

## GLOSSARY

**chaperone** (noun): an older person who goes with and takes care of a younger woman when she is in public
**edge** (noun): the outer or furthest point of something
**mainstream** (adjective): considered normal, and having or using ideas, beliefs, etc. which are accepted by most people
**trust** (noun): the belief that someone is honest and good
**immaculate** (adjective): perfectly clean or tidy
**tailor-made** (adjective): specially made for a person
**creased** (adjective): with a line on it that shows it has been ironed

# Alternatives

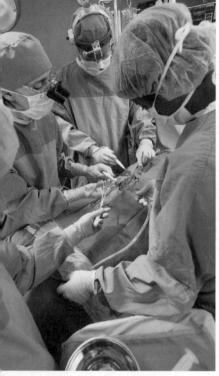

VOCABULARY

Health and treatments

VOCABULARY

Health and treatments

**1** Rearrange the letters of the words in bold to complete these definitions.

1 _____ **egrrsuy** involves cutting open the body to repair damage.

2 The result of a particular cure is its _____ **ceefft**.

3 _____ **aaegmss** is the activity of rubbing or pressing parts of someone's body in order to make their muscles relax.

4 The changes caused by a health problem are its _____ **mmopssty**.

5 _____ **aehhiopprstyy** is a way to treat muscle stiffness, pain and injury, especially by rubbing and moving the sore parts.

6 An _____ **eillnss** is a disease of the body or mind or a period of feeling ill.

7 A _____ **aeiikllnpr** is a substance used to reduce or remove physical pain.

8 A _____ **cdeeiimn** is a substance taken to treat a disease or injury.

9 _____ **accenprtuuu** is a way to treat pain and disease by positioning thin needles in the skin at special nerve centres.

10 A _____ **aeemnrttt** is the way a health problem is cured.

11 _____ **hinopsys** is a mental state like sleep, in which a person's thoughts can be easily influenced by someone else.

12 _____ **deis ceeffst** are the unpleasant consequences of a drug that are additional to its benefits.

13 A _____ **deemry** is a successful way of dealing with a health problem.

14 An _____ **abciiinott** is a drug that can destroy harmful bacteria.

15 A _____ **aacciinnotv** is given to someone to stop them getting a disease.

16 A _____ **abcelop** is a substance given to someone who is told that it is a cure for a medical problem, to make them feel as if they are getting better.

VOCABULARY

Belief and scepticism

**2** Complete the conversation using the words in the box. Use each word once.

> basis believe benefit better effects nonsense
> nothing proof tried trust works worthless

**JOHN** What's that liquid?

**LOLA** It's a Bach flower remedy. I take it for insomnia. It contains a very small amount of flower material, so you get the benefits of the flowers' energy.

**JOHN** That's [1]_____ !

**LOLA** Well it [2]_____ for me. I can see its [3]_____ when I go to bed. I sleep much better.

**JOHN** But it's [4]_____ more than a placebo, just like homeopathy.

**LOLA** Well I [5]_____ in it. Anyway, how's your attempt to give up smoking?

**JOHN** It's not easy. My doctor recommended hypnosis. I might give that a try.

**LOLA** Hypnosis! You say homeopathy's [6]_____ , but there's no [7]_____ that hypnosis works.

**JOHN** Hypnosis has been [8]_____ and tested. That's why I [9]_____ it. It's homeopathy that has no scientific [10]_____ .

**LOLA** Well as far as I understand, hypnosis is no [11]_____ than your own willpower. It offers no [12]_____ to anyone except the person you pay to hypnotise you!

## Over to you

What do you think of the two remedies mentioned in the conversation? Have you tried either of them? Did they work for you?

## GRAMMAR
*will be -ing*

**3** Complete the sentences with the *will be -ing* form of the verbs in box A and the endings in box B.

| A | B |
|---|---|
| analyse   do   lie   pass   send   snow   visit | in the sun in the Caribbean   last month's sales figures   some revision for the exam   the main sights of the city   through some turbulence   when you arrive   you a document to translate |

1 It's cold here, but this time next week you _____ .
2 At the meeting this afternoon I _____ .
3 On today's cycle tour we _____ .
4 There's cold weather on the way so it _____ .
5 Could passengers please remain seated as we _____ .
6 Check your email at about 3pm because I _____ .
7 In the next class we _____ .

## VOCABULARY
Supporting an argument

**4** Complete the words and contractions in these forum postings about different educational issues.

While I think the democratic nature of Southglen school is very positive, I'm still in favour of home-schooling. I've home-schooled my three children, and my [1]ex_____ i_____ t_____ it allows you to give each individual the attention they need. What's more, [2]ev_____ su_____ t_____ home-schooled children do as well or better in standardised tests. Some people argue that home-schooled children become isolated, but there are many ways for them to meet other children. [3]F_____ in_____ , my children go to a number of different clubs, and have plenty of friends of their own age.

Your recent article on homework confirms my own instinctive feeling that it is counter-productive. As a teacher I've [4]a_____ f_____ t_____ homework can generate a negative attitude towards studying. Now I see that [5]re_____ su_____ t_____ homework doesn't improve learning either. [6]T_____ also a lot of ev_____ t_____ homework doesn't have any of the other benefits we assign to it, [7]f_____ ex_____ , improved self-discipline and time-management skills.

I see that compulsory education until the age of 18 is on the political agenda again in this country, and I'm fully in favour of it. [8]Ex_____ h_____ sh_____ t_____ if sixteen-year-olds were offered the right courses this would benefit society. To [9]g_____ y_____ a_____ ex_____ , a young person with no academic qualifications would be offered vocational training that would teach the skills needed to find work. I left school when I was sixteen, and [10]i_____ m_____ ex_____ , finding yourself on the job market at that age with nothing to offer an employer is depressing.

## Over to you
Do you agree with the arguments in the postings? If not, what are your views on each of the issues?

**5** Read the email proposing a weekend activity for a team of employees at a company. Then put the words in the correct order to complete some employees' responses.

| Subject: | Proposal for the team activity weekend |
| --- | --- |

Our boss has suggested that we all go on a parachute jump together, and has asked me to run the idea by you and get back to her by the end of the week. The airfield is a long drive away, so it would involve staying overnight nearby. What are your thoughts?

1 reject / would / on / it / that / expensive / the proposal / the grounds / be / I'd

_____ .

2 it / strongly / be / I'd / recommend / would / doing / it / as _____

_____ an amazing experience.

3 not everyone / it / because / would / I'd / out / enjoy / rule / it _____

_____ . I know I wouldn't!

4 since / I'd / a whole weekend / it / occupy / against / advise / it / would _____

_____ .

5 I can't come unfortunately, but you, / I / it / were / for / I'd / if / go _____

_____ . It would really bring you all together!

**Over to you**

What would your reaction be to the proposal in the email? Why?

**6** Complete the description of the Spanish healthcare system using the words and phrases in the box.

> access   appointment   check-ups   choice   entitled
> free of charge   health insurance   high status   in
> information   manner   openly   out   people   treatment

I think the Spanish public healthcare system works well. The vast majority of people have access to free healthcare. As this covers every kind of [1]_____ except dental care, most people don't have private [2]_____ . Medicines aren't [3]_____ , but are cheap on prescription, and making an [4]_____ with a doctor is easy. People normally go to the doctor when they have a problem, but people in high-risk categories are encouraged to have regular [5]_____ .

Doctors have a [6]_____ in Spanish society. Patients are assigned a doctor in their area, and doctors have a friendly [7]_____ towards patients, and discuss problems and treatments [8]_____ . You're [9]_____ to change doctor if you're unhappy for some reason, but it's not an easy process. Patients aren't given [10]_____ to their medical records, though, so if you go to a private doctor, you have to explain everything again.

As for public hospitals, they work well. Patients without health insurance don't have a [11]_____ between public and private hospitals but some private hospitals collaborate with the public sector. Unless it's an emergency, hospitals don't treat [12]_____ immediately, but waiting lists are not too long. Once in hospital, patients generally stay [13]_____ wards. Most people aren't aware of how one hospital compares with another, but the government does provide [14]_____ about how good hospitals are. When a patient is home again, family members will often help [15]_____ with patient care.

HOSPITAL VIRGEN DEL MAR

**Over to you**

How does this compare with healthcare in your country?

# EXPLORE Reading

**7** If you want to laugh, what can you do? Make a list.

*watch a comedy series on TV, ...*

**8** Do you think these sentences are true or false? Read the article to check your answers. How many of the things from your list in Exercise 7 does it include?

| | |
|---|---|
| 1 Laughing can be bad for your health. | TRUE / FALSE |
| 2 There are different types of laughter. | TRUE / FALSE |
| 3 Some people go to special clubs to laugh with other people. | TRUE / FALSE |
| 4 Scientists can't explain how laughing produces changes in our body. | TRUE / FALSE |

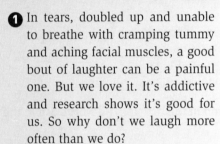

# Laugh? I feel better already

**As gloom dominates the news, the best remedy could be a good giggle – and it's also good for your health.**

**❶** In tears, doubled up and unable to breathe with cramping tummy and aching facial muscles, a good bout of laughter can be a painful one. But we love it. It's addictive and research shows it's good for us. So why don't we laugh more often than we do?

**❷** As stress, anxiety and tension increase, mirth wanes and it becomes more difficult to find things funny. But help is out there. Through laughter-yoga clubs, clown workshops and comedy courses, funny seminars, self-help humour books and laughing tapes, we can discover what kind of humour we respond to best. Everybody is different.

**❸** The health and social benefits of laughter sparked the interest of Dr Madan Kataria in Mumbai, India. He believes that there are two kinds of laughter: humour, which requires certain intellectual and communication skills not available to everybody; and inner laughter, which is more emotional, childlike and accessible to all. 'Children don't have a great sense of humour,' he says, 'they don't need jokes to laugh. They laugh because they feel like it.'

**❹** Based on this idea of inner laughter, Kataria developed his philosophies and exercises of laughter-yoga and meditation. 'Seeking to connect the outer, more physical, act of laughter with the inner, more emotional one,' he says. 'This is the philosophy of laughter-yoga.'

**❺** A successful laughter club requires group effort. There is a lot of body language and eye contact done in the laughter exercises, which is important for removing mental blocks and social inhibitions. It may not be everybody's idea of a good guffaw, but laughter is certainly infectious and tends to spread rapidly with eye contact.

**❻** Julie Whitehead, a yoga teacher, hosts a laughter club every month. She stresses that people who turn up to the session must come willing to laugh. Following Kataria's philosophies, she tells everyone to 'Fake it, fake it, until you make it.' Our body doesn't know the difference between real and fake laughter, providing one does it convincingly. Our bodies, not sensing the difference, still release the same healthy chemicals.

**❼** Dr Lee S Berk, a researcher in psychoneuroimmunology (PNI) at Loma Linda University, California, is involved in producing scientific evidence of these happy hormones, something Dr Kataria has been following since he began developing his laughter-yoga philosophy. Berk initially had doubts that his findings would be medically accepted. 'But the reality is that now there's a real science to the health benefits of laughter,' Berk says. 'And it's as real as taking a drug.'

Visit **www.laughteryoga.co.uk** for more information.

**9**   In which paragraph(s) of the article can you read about ...

1   how laughter-yoga was developed?  _____

2   the acceptance of laughter's benefits by the medical community?  _____

3   the differences between laughter in adults and children?  _____

4   the attitude needed to make a laughter club work well?  _____

5   our physical reactions during a good laugh?  _____

6   why we don't laugh more?  _____

**10**   Circle the best answer to these questions.

1   What does Dr Kataria say about laughter?
a   Humour is a type of laughter that all adults can enjoy.
b   Children don't laugh at jokes because they don't have a sense of humour.
c   All adults and children can enjoy inner laughter.

2   What does Dr Kataria aim to do through laughter-yoga?
a   Help people to experience laughter both physically and emotionally.
b   Connect humour and inner laughter.
c   Develop new yoga exercises and meditation techniques.

3   What does the article say about laughter at laughter clubs?
a   Some people don't laugh because of social inhibitions.
b   Eye contact is vital for getting everyone laughing.
c   You only get its benefits if it's real.

4   What do we find out about Julie Whitehead's laughter club?
a   She uses the same exercises as Dr Kataria uses.
b   It doesn't work unless people come prepared to laugh.
c   It works thanks to her effort to make people laugh.

**11**   Find words with a similar or opposite meaning in the article. The words are in the same order as they appear in the article.

**With a similar meaning:**

1   laugh, _____ , _____

2   laughter, _____

3   cramping, _____ , _____

4   available, _____

5   _____ , come

**With the opposite meaning:**

6   increases _____

7   intellectual _____

8   inner _____

9   real _____

---

## GLOSSARY

**gloom** (noun): feelings of great unhappiness and loss of hope
**double up** (verb): to bend suddenly forwards and down, usually because of pain or laughter
**bout** (noun): a short period of involvement in an activity

**1** Before you watch, answer these questions about alternative medicine.

|  |  | Me | Leo | Anna Laura |
|---|---|---|---|---|
| 1 | Do you generally believe in alternative medicine? |  |  |  |
| 2 | Have you tried an alternative therapy or remedy? |  |  |  |
| 3 | If so, what have you tried? |  |  |  |
| 4 | Were you satisfied with the results? |  |  |  |

**2** Watch the video and complete the table for Leo and Anna Laura.

**3** Watch Leo again (0:11–1:32) and answer the questions.

Leo    Anna Laura

1 Where did Leo grow up?
2 What was his experience of alternative medicine before the events he describes?
3 What problem were he and his wife having?
4 Why did they consult an acupuncture doctor?
5 What was a possible cause of the problem?
6 How did Leo feel when he started the treatment?

**4** Complete the words in these extracts from the video in which Leo talks about the medical process he went through. Watch again to check if necessary.

1 When we g_____ s_____, we usually go to see a modern doctor.
2 We had numerous m_____ c_____-u_____.
3 As a l_____ r_____, we went to c_____ a Chinese acupuncture doctor.
4 I ... felt the problem could r_____ to stress or hormonal imbalances, and that's where acupuncture could c_____ i_____.
5 We started our first c_____ of t_____.

**5** Watch Anna Laura again (1:36–2:34). Are the sentences true or false? Correct the false ones.

1 Anna Laura doesn't generally use alternative remedies.      TRUE / FALSE
2 Her sister is very keen on alternative medicine.            TRUE / FALSE
3 She tried a homeopathic remedy out of curiosity.           TRUE / FALSE
4 Anna Laura was bitten by a mosquito.                       TRUE / FALSE
5 The bite caused an allergic reaction.                      TRUE / FALSE
6 The cream didn't work very quickly.                        TRUE / FALSE

**6** Complete these extracts from the video with a preposition. Watch again to check if necessary.

1 I myself am not particularly _____ alternative medicine.
2 I'm quite sceptical _____ these things.
3 We were _____ holiday in Italy.
4 My husband is allergic _____ mosquito bites.
5 We were converted _____ thinking that homeopathy did seem to work.

**7** If you are sceptical about alternative medicine, have Leo and Anna Laura's experiences made you think again? If you believe in alternative medicine, how would you try to convince someone who is sceptical?

## GLOSSARY

**GP** (noun): General Practitioner: a doctor who provides general medical treatment for people in a particular area
**hormonal** (adjective): relating to hormones (chemicals made by living cells which influence the development of a person)
**imbalance** (noun): when things which should be equal, or are normally equal, are not
**last resort** (noun): the only alternative left when all other methods fail
**sceptical** (adjective): doubting that something is true or useful
**allergic** (adjective): causing a condition that makes a person become ill or develop skin or breathing problems
**rash** (noun): a lot of small red spots on the skin
**itching** (noun): an uncomfortable feeling on the skin which makes you want to rub it with your nails
**staggering** (adjective): very surprising

# 13 Compromise

**VOCABULARY**
Disagreement and compromise

**1** Complete the expressions of disagreement and compromise using the verbs in the box. Use each verb once.

| call | get | have | make | organise (x2) | propose (x2) | take (x2) | talk | thrash |
|------|-----|------|------|---------------|--------------|-----------|------|--------|

1  ___*have*___ a word with (someone)
2  _____ everyone's opinion
3  _____ an alternative
4  _____ a formal complaint
5  _____ a petition
6  _____ a compromise
7  _____ legal advice
8  _____ a demonstration
9  _____ (something) out
10 _____ a meeting
11 _____ (something) over
12 _____ legal action

**2** Complete the letters with expressions from Exercise 1. Use each expression once.

Dear Mrs Campbell,

I wanted to ¹_____ you about the plans to turn the supermarket on the corner into a nightclub, but haven't managed to catch you at home. We would obviously be the people most affected by the plans, but I'd like to know what other people think, so I think it would be a good idea to ²_____ before we do anything else. I don't mind knocking on doors to speak to people. If others are unhappy too, we could ³_____ at the community centre to discuss what action to take. I was thinking that to start with we could ⁴_____ to the council, and then ⁵_____ for people in the neighbourhood to sign. If that doesn't work, maybe we could ⁶_____ and block the traffic in the main road. Please let me know what you think.

Best regards,
Marco Tomasetti

Dear Marco,

I have indeed heard about the plans, and agree that we should do something. But let's take things one step at a time. Maybe we need to ⁷_____ first. My brother-in-law's a lawyer, so he'd be able to tell us if we can ⁸_____ to prevent the plan from going ahead, though I suspect that we may need to ⁹_____ that leaves both sides happy. I imagine the council has already made a decision to have a nightclub there, so they're not going to ¹⁰_____ at this point. So we'll just have to ¹¹_____ an agreement _____ and hope it solves our problems. We could insist that they invest in the best possible soundproofing, for example. Let me ¹²_____ this _____ with my brother-in-law first, though, and I'll get back to you.

Yours,
Mary Campbell

## Over to you

What do you think is the best way to deal with the problem discussed in the letters?

**3** Jared is talking to his boss, Meva, about the use of space in the office. Complete their conversation using the words in the box.

> about (x3)  afraid  any  been  besides  case (x2)  forgetting
> know  problem  that  thinking  thought

**MEVA** Jared. You wanted to see me.

**JARED** Yes. It's about trying to find an area for us all to have lunch in.

**MEVA** You ¹_____ what I think about that. I'm ²_____ we just don't have space. And ³_____, I'm not sure it's really necessary.

**JARED** I disagree. We're all fed up with eating in front of our computers. And we need somewhere we can chat without disturbing other people.

**MEVA** So what do you suggest?

**JARED** Well, I've ⁴_____ ⁵_____. What ⁶_____ the old storeroom?

**MEVA** Aren't you ⁷_____ ⁸_____ all the stuff that's in there? And in ⁹_____ ¹⁰_____, it's very small and dark.

**JARED** That's no ¹¹_____. If we put up some shelves in the new storeroom, there would be space for everything there. Then we could decorate it. We only need space for a table and a few chairs.

**MEVA** It's not as easy as it sounds. Who's going to buy the shelves? Who's going to put them up? And move everything? We don't have the time or money to get that done.

**JARED** I've already ¹²_____ ¹³_____ that. If the company is prepared to buy the shelves, we'll put them up and do all the work in our own time.

**MEVA** In ¹⁴_____ ¹⁵_____, I'm willing to consider it.

**4** Find and correct one error in each sentence. The error could be a wrong word, an extra word or wrong word order.

Tom

Liv

**1** If you ignore a difficult problem, it will usually go off.

**2** The only way to deal with a difficult problem is to face up it to.

**3** The key to a successful relationship is learning to put up for your partner's annoying habits.

**4** To make a relationship work, it's important to speak over the things that annoy you.

**5** For a new company to work, you just need to come up a good idea with.

**6** You should always carry out plenty of market research before you consider setting in a new company.

**7** It's best to leave negotiations for another day if they break them down.

**8** For negotiations to succeed, it's important to keep of the pressure on the other side.

**5** Replace the <u>underlined</u> verb phrases with a multi-word verb. Use the correct form of the verbs in the box and a preposition and/or adverb. Change the word order if necessary. Use each verb once.

> break   bring   come   go   set   sit   sort   talk

### Mediation report

**Participants:** Adila Kenyatta and Mirna Ostrowski

We ¹<u>organised</u> a mediation session for 10am and both parties arrived punctually. Adila came with her sister, Kabisa, and Mirna ²<u>was accompanied by</u> her husband, Erik. For much of the time, both sides spoke openly about the problem and ³<u>discussed it</u> calmly, and at one point seemed close to ⁴<u>finding</u> a solution. However, there are still major differences in the way the two sides interpret the cause of the conflict, and they couldn't find a way to ⁵<u>solve them</u>. Unfortunately, communication started to ⁶<u>fail</u> here, and both sides agreed that the session had ⁷<u>lasted</u> long enough for one day. They agreed to ⁸<u>meet</u> again at the same time next week to continue working on a solution.

1 _____   5 _____
2 _____   6 _____
3 _____   7 _____
4 _____   8 _____

**Over to you**

In Exercise 4, who do you generally agree with, Tom or Liv? Are there any of the person's opinions you do *not* agree with? Explain why.

**VOCABULARY**
Negotiating an agreement

**6** Complete the words in this conversation between a shop owner and a builder.

HUGO  I ¹ga_____ you're not happy with the work.

AMAIA  It's not the work, it's the fact that you didn't finish on time. We think we should ²b_____ co_____ f_____ that.

HUGO  What exactly did you ³h_____ i_____ m_____ ?

AMAIA  We think we're ⁴en_____ t_____ a significant discount on the final cost. Let's say 25%.

HUGO  We only finished two days late. I don't ⁵ho_____ s_____ w_____ we should give you a 25% discount. There was no penalty clause in our contract.

AMAIA  But you knew the opening day was last Saturday. We had to cancel that and we'd already paid for publicity, entertainment and fresh snacks for all our customers.

HUGO  And we're ⁶pre_____ t_____ cover those costs. But I'm ⁷a_____ we c_____ ag_____ t_____ a 25% discount on the job.

AMAIA  But we'll have to pay out that money all over again when we finally open. We ⁸pr_____ that you pay those costs too.

HUGO  We'd ⁹b_____ wi_____ t_____ cover all your opening day costs ¹⁰pr_____ you agree to pay the refitting costs in full.

AMAIA  I don't ¹¹th_____ we c_____ ac_____ that. Surely you should take some responsibility for finishing your work late.

HUGO  This is the first of a chain of shops you're planning to open, right?

AMAIA  That's right, although exactly how many we open ¹²de_____ o_____ how well this one goes.

HUGO  We ¹³c_____ of_____ a 25% discount on this job if you contract us for fitting out the rest of the shops you open.

AMAIA  OK, we'll consider that. I'll talk to the others and get back to you.

**Over to you**

Do you think that the agreement reached in the conversation is a good one? Why? / Why not?

# EXPLORE Writing

**7** Read this email from a university tutor about a dispute between a student and one of her teachers. Then answer the questions.

1 Has the tutor made any progress in resolving the dispute?
2 Does he believe one side in the dispute more than the other?
3 How do you think the dispute could be resolved?

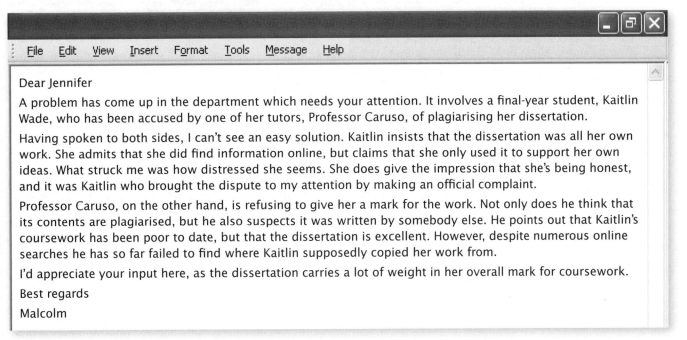

File   Edit   View   Insert   Format   Tools   Message   Help

Dear Jennifer

A problem has come up in the department which needs your attention. It involves a final-year student, Kaitlin Wade, who has been accused by one of her tutors, Professor Caruso, of plagiarising her dissertation.

Having spoken to both sides, I can't see an easy solution. Kaitlin insists that the dissertation was all her own work. She admits that she did find information online, but claims that she only used it to support her own ideas. What struck me was how distressed she seems. She does give the impression that she's being honest, and it was Kaitlin who brought the dispute to my attention by making an official complaint.

Professor Caruso, on the other hand, is refusing to give her a mark for the work. Not only does he think that its contents are plagiarised, but he also suspects it was written by somebody else. He points out that Kaitlin's coursework has been poor to date, but that the dissertation is excellent. However, despite numerous online searches he has so far failed to find where Kaitlin supposedly copied her work from.

I'd appreciate your input here, as the dissertation carries a lot of weight in her overall mark for coursework.

Best regards

Malcolm

**8** <u>Underline</u> seven verbs in Malcolm's email that are used to report what the people said. Which one tells us that the speaker ...

1 puts a lot of emphasis on what he or she said? _____

2 uses what he or she said as evidence to support his or her opinion? _____

3 thinks something could be true, but can't prove it? _____

**9** These sentences reflect what Malcolm says, but in his email he uses more emphasis. Can you remember how he adds emphasis? Read the email again to check your answers.

1 She admits that she found information online.
2 I was struck by how distressed she seems.
3 She gives the impression that she's being honest.
4 Kaitlin brought the dispute to my attention.
5 He thinks that its contents are plagiarised and he also suspects it was written by somebody else.

**10** Look at these notes about a dispute, or think about / invent another one related to your studies or work. Write an email describing the dispute and report what the two sides say. If possible, suggest a solution. Include some of the verbs from Exercise 7 and the techniques for adding emphasis in Exercises 8 and 9.

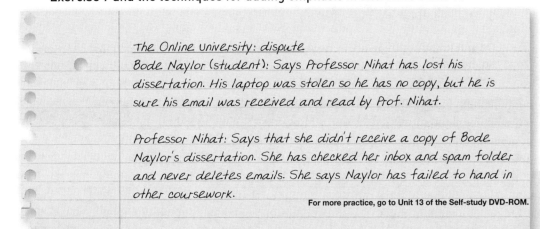

The Online University: dispute

Bode Naylor (student): Says Professor Nihat has lost his dissertation. His laptop was stolen so he has no copy, but he is sure his email was received and read by Prof. Nihat.

Professor Nihat: Says that she didn't receive a copy of Bode Naylor's dissertation. She has checked her inbox and spam folder and never deletes emails. She says Naylor has failed to hand in other coursework.

For more practice, go to Unit 13 of the Self-study DVD-ROM.

1    **Before you watch, think about these questions.**

Do you have any experience of negotiating in a work or study context? What were the negotiations about? Were they successful? If not, why not?

Andrés                Di

2    **Watch the video. Who talks about these things?**
(Circle) *Andrés*, *Di*, or *BOTH*.

1    Cultural differences            ANDRÉS / DI / BOTH
2    Accepted ways of doing things   ANDRÉS / DI / BOTH
3    Making changes                  ANDRÉS / DI / BOTH
4    Misunderstandings               ANDRÉS / DI / BOTH

3    **Watch Andrés again (0:11–1:10) and answer the questions.**

1    Where was Andrés working? Be specific.
2    What basic change did Andrés want to make to working methods?
3    How did people react to these changes at first? Why?
4    What compromise did Andrés suggest?
5    What did people have to do as a result of the compromise?
6    What were the results of the changes that Andrés introduced?
7    What did people want to do as a result of the changes?

4    **Complete these extracts from what Andrés says about workplace negotiating. Write one word in each gap. Watch again to check if necessary.**

**Before the compromise**

'People are $^1$_____ to doing things a different way, which is waking up in the morning and going where they $^2$_____ , shooting what they $^3$_____ .'

**How he presented the compromise**

'I said OK, let's do it this way, $^4$_____ of doing the planning ahead $^5$_____ just try a couple of weeks with $^6$_____ for resources, vehicles and cameras.'

**The result of the compromise**

'After a couple of weeks of … just $^7$_____ me know where they're going, … people $^8$_____ to be happier.'

5    **Watch Di again talking about Western versus Eastern negotiating styles (1:14–2:34) and** (circle) **the best option to complete the sentences.**

1    There are some / big differences in how people negotiate and compromise in Western and Eastern cultures.
2    In Eastern culture, decisions are often / generally not made during meetings.
3    In Eastern culture, final decisions are decided in smaller groups / another meeting.
4    In meetings between Eastern and Western business people, the two sides often have similar / different opinions about how a meeting went.
5    Di says that Chinese people will always agree / seem to agree with Westerners during meetings.

6    **What is Di referring to when he says these things? Watch again if necessary.**

1    it's pretty hard
2    it's more likely
3    things are more direct
4    things can be great
5    the result can be quite different

7    **Do you know anything about negotiating in other parts of the world, for example Africa or South America? If so, how does it compare to negotiating in Western and Eastern cultures? If not, look on the Internet to see if you can find any information about it.**

**GLOSSARY**

**shoot** (verb): to use a camera to record a film
**flow** (noun): the movement of something in one direction
**ally** (noun): someone who helps and supports someone else

# 14 Changes

**VOCABULARY**

Predicting the future

**1** Match the sentence halves to complete these predictions about the future.

**TRANSPORT**
1 We'll see ...
2 I predict that ...

**CLIMATE**
3 We could very well ...
4 The next step could be ...

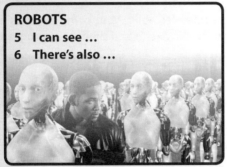

**ROBOTS**
5 I can see ...
6 There's also ...

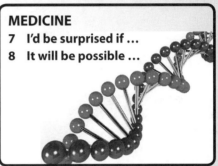

**MEDICINE**
7 I'd be surprised if ...
8 It will be possible ...

a robots doing all manual jobs.
b have complete control over the weather.
c we don't have a cure for all major diseases.
d cars that run on compressed air.
e the possibility that robots will fight our wars.
f to replace all body parts.
g adapting local climates to people's needs.
h air travel will be very expensive.

**2** Which predictions ...

a express the highest level of certainty?  ___ , ___

b express the lowest level of certainty?  ___ , ___ , ___

**VOCABULARY**

Future time expressions

**3** It's the year 2020 and Michelle is 20 years old. Match the future time expressions (1–7) with the expressions in the box. There may be more than one correct answer.

by the mid-2020s   in the future   by 2030   in about 2040
by the end of the century   before long   in the long term

1 in about ten years = _____

2 in about twenty years' time = _____

3 Looking ahead, ... = _____

4 Further into the future = _____

5 in the short term = _____

6 within a few years = _____

7 within my lifetime = _____

Michelle

**Over to you**

Do you think the predictions in Exercise 1 will come true? If so, when? Use expressions from Exercise 3 in your answers.

GRAMMAR
Future progressive and future perfect

**4** Complete the article about young people in the UK using *will* and the future progressive or future perfect form of the verbs in brackets.

Society in the UK is changing rapidly, and teenagers today are likely to lead markedly different lives from those of their parents or grandparents. If we look at the statistics for women, an average teenager today ¹_____ (leave) home by the time she's 24, about a year earlier than a man. In fact, one in three of her male friends ²_____ (live) at home when they are thirty. Employment figures by sector suggest that she ³_____ (work) in an administrative or secretarial role. As for having her own family, if she decides to be a mother, she ⁴_____ (have) her first child by the age of 28. However, she ⁵_____ (cohabit) with her partner and ⁶_____ (not get) married. Although the majority of UK families are currently headed by a married couple, married couples represent a minority of younger people. She and her partner ⁷_____ (rent) accommodation at this stage, but they ⁸_____ (buy) their own home by their mid-thirties. Almost 70% of Britons own their home and the average age of a first-time house buyer is 34.

**5** Write complete sentences about your own future using *will*, *won't*, *may*, *might*, *should*, *hope to* or *would like to* and the future progressive or future perfect.

1  I / move to a new house / by the end of next year

_____

2  I / sleep / at midnight tonight

_____

3  I / work / when I'm 65

_____

4  I / stop driving for ecological reasons / by 2030

_____

5  I / take up a new hobby / by this time next year

_____

6  I / study English / in five years' time

_____

7  I / have a holiday in space / by 2050

_____

8  I / run my own business / in ten years from now

_____

Over to you

Is the article in Exercise 4 true of young people in your country? If not, write about any differences.

VOCABULARY
Interview questions

**6** Complete the questions in this job interview with a word from each box, A and B.

| A | B |
|---|---|
| confident   contributions   hope   how   intend   reasons   what   would | achieved   doing   for   handle   make   say   that   to |

**DREW**  What are your ¹_____ _____ applying for this job?

**HARUN**  I've been teaching for years, and I think I'm ready to move into a management role.

**DREW**  Many of our teachers are employed in the English department. Are you ²_____ _____ you have the level of English required?

**HARUN**  Definitely. I studied English at university and I use English on a daily basis.

**DREW**  What ³_____ will you _____ to the way things are done?

**HARUN**  I have a lot of ideas. For example, I'd like to organise more in-house training.

## Over to you

Think of a job you would like to do. Which questions in Exercise 6 would you expect to be asked at an interview for the job? Write your answers to these questions.

**DREW** What do you [4]_____ to have _____ by the end of this academic year?

**HARUN** I hope to have spoken to and observed all teachers so as to find out what type of training and support would be most beneficial.

**DREW** You have a young family. [5]_____ will you _____ the long working hours and late finishes?

**HARUN** Both kids are at school now, so I don't see that as a problem.

**DREW** People don't tend to stay long in this job. What do you [6]_____ _____ do when you finally decide to move on?

**HARUN** Right now I have no intention of moving on. I've been a teacher here for ten years, so I know how things work.

**DREW** But [7]_____ do you think you'll be _____ in ten years' time?

**HARUN** I prefer to think about the present. You never quite know what the future will bring.

**DREW** And what [8]_____ you _____ are the qualities that make you a good candidate?

**HARUN** I'm organised, I'm well trained, and I like working with people.

---

**VOCABULARY**

Recruitment

**7** Complete the words in this mini-dictionary of recruitment terms.

## The A to Z of recruitment

1 **c**_ _ _ _ _ _ _ _ _ (n) a person who is in the selection process for a job

2 **c**_ _ _ _ _ _ _ _ _**l**_ _ _ _ _ (n) a document that explains why you are applying for a particular job (**cover ~** in US English)

3 **C**_ (n) a one- or two-page document detailing your qualifications and the jobs you have had

4 **e**_ _ _ _ _ _ _ _ _ _ _ (n) the knowledge and skills you gain by doing a job

5 **g**_ _ _ _ _ _ (n) a person who has completed their university or college studies

6 **i**_ _ _ _ _ _ _ _ _ _ (n) a period of training you do after studying in order to qualify to work in a particular job

7 **i**_ _ _ _ _ _ _ _ _ _**s**_ _ _ _ (n) the part of the selection process for a job in which an employer speaks to possible employees

8 **n**_ _ _ _ _ **g**_ _ _ _ _ _ _ _ (adj) recently finished at university or college

9 **m**_ _ _ _ **o**_ _ _ _ _ _ _ _ _ (n) the thing that you most hope to achieve in a job

10 **p**_ _ _ _ _ _ _ _ _ _ (n) the study of a person's personality and behaviour

11 **r**_ _ _ _ _ _ _ _ _ _ (n pl) written statements from a teacher (**academic ~**) or an employer (**professional ~**) that confirm information you give to an employer

12 **s**_ _ _ _ _ _ (n) a fixed quantity of money that you earn each month for doing a job

13 **s**_ _ _ _**y**_ _ _ _ _ _ _ _ (v) persuade somebody that you have a lot of positive qualities

14 **s**_ _ _ _ _ (n) the way an interview is conducted, e.g. in a **conversational** or a **formal ~**

15 **s**_ _ _ _ _ _ (v) send by mail, email or by completing an online application form

# EXPLOREReading

8    Look at these threats to life on our planet and answer the questions.

- Meteorite impact  • Viral pandemic  • Take-over by robots
- Climate change  • Nuclear war  • Eruption of super-volcano

1    Which one do you think is most likely to occur during our lifetime?
2    Which one do you think would have the biggest impact on life on our planet?

9    Quickly read the article, in which scientists talk about the major threats to life on our planet. Which two threats in Exercise 8 are *not* mentioned?

# What a way to go

How will it all end? Below, four scientists talk about their greatest fears and explain how society could be affected. After each one, we estimate the chance of the threat occurring in our lifetime (over the next 70 years), and the danger that it would pose to the human race if it did happen (10 = making humans extinct).

**Nick Brooks**, senior research associate at the Tyndall Centre for Climate Change Research:

**Threat 1**

'By the end of this century it is likely that greenhouse gases will have doubled and the average global temperature will have risen by at least 2°C. This is hotter than anything the Earth has experienced in the last one and a half million years. In the worst case scenario it could completely alter the climate in many regions of the world. This could lead to global food insecurity and the widespread collapse of existing social systems, causing mass migration and conflict over resources [1]___ .'

**Threat 2**

**Air Marshal Lord Garden**, author of *Can Deterrence Last?*:

'In theory, a nuclear war could destroy the human civilisation but in practice I think the time of that danger has probably passed. There are three potential nuclear flashpoints today: the Middle East, India–Pakistan and North Korea. But I like to believe the barriers against using a nuclear weapon remain high because of the way we have developed an international system to restrain nuclear use. The probability of nuclear war on a global scale is low [2]___ .'

**Donald Yeomans**, manager of NASA's Near Earth Object Program Office:

**Threat 3**

'To cause a serious setback to our civilisation, an impactor would have to be around 1.5km wide or larger. We expect an event of this type every million years on average. The dangers associated with such a large impactor include an enormous amount of dust in the atmosphere, which would substantially shut down sunlight for weeks, thus affecting plant life and crops that sustain life. All of these effects are relatively short-term [3]___ .'

**Threat 4**

**Professor Bill McGuire**, director of the Benfield Hazard Research Centre:

'Approximately every 50,000 years the Earth experiences a super-volcano. More than 1,000 sq km of land can be obliterated, the surrounding continent is coated in ash, and sulphur gases are injected into the atmosphere, reflecting back sunlight for years to come. A super-volcano is 12 times more likely than a large meteorite impact. Places to watch now are those that have erupted in the past, such as Yellowstone in the US and Toba. But, even more worryingly, a super-volcano could also burst out from somewhere that has never erupted before [4]___ .'

10 Read the article more carefully. Circle the correct chance or danger score for each threat.

| Threat 1 | Chance = [1]**low / high** | Danger score = 6 |
| Threat 2 | Chance = low | Danger score = [2]**5 / 8** |
| Threat 3 | Chance = medium | Danger score = [3]**5 / 10** |
| Threat 4 | Chance = [4]**low / very high** | Danger score = 7 |

11 Match the extracts (a–d) from the article with the gaps (1–4). Write the number of the correct gap in the box.

a   ... , even if there remains the possibility of nuclear use by a rogue state or fanatical extremists ☐

b   ... , such as under the Amazon rainforest ☐

c   ... as some parts of the world become much less habitable ☐

d   ... , so the most adaptable species (cockroaches and humans, for example) would be likely to survive ☐

12 Answer the questions about the different threats mentioned in the article. Write the number of the correct threat.

1   In which case is it impossible to be sure where the problem will occur? ☐

2   Which threat is less likely to destroy our civilisation today than it was in the past? ☐

3   Which threat could lead to fighting or wars? ☐

4   Which threat would we probably recover from most quickly? ☐

5   Which threat have we taken successful steps to avoid? ☐

6   Which threat would leave the Earth in relative darkness for a very long period? ☐

13 Find words or expressions in the article to complete these definitions.

1   The _____ is the most unpleasant or serious thing which could happen in a situation. (Threat 1)

2   If something exists or happens in a lot of places, it is _____ . (Threat 1)

3   _____ are places at which violence might be expected to begin. (Threat 2)

4   If something happens _____ , it affects the whole world. (Threat 2)

5   A _____ is something that happens which delays or prevents a process from advancing. (Threat 3)

6   If something is _____ , all signs of it have been removed by destroying it. (Threat 4)

7   To _____ means to break through a surface and come out with great force. (Threat 4)

**Over to you**

Which of the threats in the article are you most concerned about? Do you think any of them are given too much or too little attention in the media?

## Before you watch

1    Do the Antarctic quiz.

Magda

# The Antarctic Quiz

**How much do you know about Antarctica? Test your knowledge with this quiz. Circle the correct answers.**

1    The <u>North Pole</u> / <u>South Pole</u> is in Antarctica.
2    The hole in the ozone layer <u>was</u> / <u>wasn't</u> discovered in Antarctica.
3    Scientists <u>can</u> / <u>cannot</u> study glaciers in Antarctica.
4    Penguins <u>live</u> / <u>don't live</u> in Antarctica.
5    Antarctica is the <u>driest</u> / <u>wettest</u> continent in the world.
6    Antarctica has <u>no</u> / <u>very few</u> human inhabitants.

## While you watch

2    Watch the video and check your answers to the quiz. Which question isn't answered in the video?

3    Watch Part 1 again (0:07–1:15). Note down these things.

    1   Where Magda comes from: _____

    2   The name of the science of making maps: _____

    3   Her job at the BAS: _____

    4   Three different ways of visualising Antarctica that she works with: _____

    5   Three different things the maps she makes show: _____

4    BAS stands for British Antarctic Survey. What do MAGIC and GIS stand for? Watch the first part again if necessary.

    MAGIC    _____

    GIS        _____

5    Watch Part 2 again (1:15–2:29) and answer the questions.

    1   What does Magda say about the importance of the BAS in Antarctica?
    2   How long has the BAS been present there?
    3   When did the BAS discover the hole in the ozone layer?
    4   What three areas of scientific research does she mention?
    5   What roles do BAS's two ships have?
    6   What can be put under the planes instead of wheels? For what purpose?

6   Watch Part 3 again (2:29–3:59) and complete the sentences.

1   Magda's colleague realised that on satellite images he could see _____ .
2   He looked at other satellite images to check _____ .
3   In total he located _____ .
4   This was an amazing discovery because _____ .
5   Last season they _____ .
6   In Cambridge, people are now _____ .

7   Watch Part 4 again (3:59–5:07) and complete the fact file about Magda.

> Name: Magda Biszczuk
> Started work at BAS: [1]_____
> Number of trips to Antarctica: [2]_____
> Future plans: [3]_____
> Most memorable moment: [4]_____
> Opinion of her job at BAS: [5]_____

# After you watch

8   Look at these extracts from the video. First, decide what you think the underlined words mean from the context. Then write them next to the correct definitions (a–f) below.

1   He found big stains on the ice, and he realised actually this is the penguin poo and of the Emperor penguins.
2   It's such a high resolution on the image we can distinguish between chicks and between the adults.
3   Antarctica that is the, the highest, the windiest, the most remote and the driest continent in the world and it's completely unspoilt.
4   Doesn't have any human inhabitant just only wildlife.

a   a long way from any towns or cities: _____
b   animals and plants that grow independently of people, usually in natural conditions: _____
c   a baby bird: _____
d   beautiful because it has not been changed or damaged by people: _____
e   a dirty mark on something: _____
f   the number of pixels (individual points of colour) contained in a picture: _____

9   What did you learn about Antarctica from doing these activities that you didn't know before? Would you like to work there? Why? / Why not?

## GLOSSARY

**ozone layer** (noun): a layer of air high above the Earth, which contains a lot of ozone, and which prevents harmful ultraviolet light from the sun from reaching the Earth
**glacier** (noun): a large mass of ice which moves slowly
**terrain** (noun): an area of land, when considering its natural features
**penguin poo** (noun): penguin excrement (remains of food from the body)
**colony** (noun): a group of animals of the same type that live together

# Acknowledgements

**The authors** would like to thank the editorial team in Cambridge, particularly Greg Sibley. Thanks, too, to Will Capel in his role as project manager for making the writing process such a trouble-free experience, and to Sally Cooke for her ever-thorough copy-editing.

**Rob Metcalf** would like to thank Anna, Eric and Sergi for their patience and support.

**Chris Cavey** would like to thank Kate, Lily and Ella for their patience and support.

**Alison Greenwood** would like to thank Beppe for all his help and support, and Hely and Rich for putting up with her.

**The authors and publishers are also grateful to the following contributors:**

Text design and page make-up: Stephanie White at Kamae Design

Picture research: Hilary Luckcock

**The authors and publishers acknowledge the following sources of copyright material and are grateful for the permissions granted. While every effort has been made, it has not always been possible to identify the sources of all the material used, or to trace all copyright holders. If any omissions are brought to our notice, we will be happy to include the appropriate acknowledgements on reprinting.**

For the text on p23 'Machu Picchu … Lost City of the Incas' adapted from http://www.machu-picchu.info/history.htm; Pamela A. Lewis for the text on p46 'Immobile on the phone' reproduced with permission of Pamela A. Lewis; The Guardian for the adapted article on p59 'Space exploration volunteers wanted (The catch? It's a one-way ticket)' by Daniel Nasaw and Andy Duckworth, *The Guardian* 19.07.09. Copyright Guardian News & Media Ltd 2009; Alex Murphy for the text on p69 'Laugh? I feel better already' first published in *The Guardian* on 25.03.03; Kate Ravilious for the extract on p80 'What a way to go' first published in *The Guardian* on 14.04.05. Reproduced with permission.

**The publisher has used its best endeavours to ensure that the URLs for external websites referred to in this book are correct and active at the time of going to press. However, the publisher has no responsibility for the websites and can make no guarantee that a site will remain live or that the content is or will remain appropriate.**

**The publishers are grateful to the following for the permissions to reproduce**

**copyright photographs and material:**

Key: l = left, c = centre, r = right, t = top, b = bottom

Alamy/©Richard Green for p4(t), /©Bill Bachmann for p4(b), /©Profimedia International s.r.o. for p10(t), /©Peter Stone for p11(b), /©Itanistock for p17(cr), /©David Levenson for p20(t), /©Danita Delimont for p20(b), /©Dean Mitchell for p28(b), /©Nordicphotos for p32(tl), /©Eye Ubiquitous for p32(tr), /©Form Advertising for p32(b), /©Jeremy Hoare for p33, /©Glow Asia RF for p38(r), /©By Ian Miles – Flashpoint Pictures for p39(l), /©Rohit Seth for p51(t), /©George Munday for p51(b), /©Interfoto for p56(b), /©Horizon International Images Ltd for p59(t), /©Stocktrek Images Inc for p59(b), /©imagebroker for p61(b), /©Adam James for p68, /©Image Source for p69, /©I love images for p73(br), /©GoGo Images Corporation for p74, /©Finnbarr Webster for p77(tr), /©Jennie Hart for p80(t), /©Greg Vaughn for p80(b); Corbis/©Hulton Deutsch Collection for p21(t), /©Bettmann for p21(c), /©Ariel Ramerez for p21(b), /©FILES/epa for p22(t), /©The Art Archive for p26(t), /©Bettmann for p80(cl); Delta Haze Corporation for p57; Edison Caetano for p55(b); Education Photos for p16; Getty Images/©Photodisc for p17(t), Asia Images Group for p17(cl), /©Knauer/Johnston for p17(b), /©Photodisc for p34(t), /©Comstock for p34(b), /©Asia Images Group for p35, /©Photodisc for p44(b), /©Time & Life Pictures for p56(t), /©Loop Delay for p73(bl), /©Altrendo Images for p78(t); istockphoto/©Ke Wang for p11(c), /©Stephen Rees for p14(l), /©Vyacheslav Shramko for p15(c), /©Jacob Wackerhausen for p15(b), /©Lisa F Young for p19(tr), /©Cheryl Casey for p19(cr), /©Robert Brown for p19(2), /©Amy Harris for p23(t), /©dejan suc for p25(cr), /©narvikk for p25(r), /©Oleksii Baliura for p26(b), /©DSG pro for p27, /©Ryan Klos for p32(cl), /©ad_doward for p38(l), /©Martin Mcelligott for p39(r), /©Marcus Clackson for p40, /©Eugene Coi for p43(t), /©Gene Chutka for p45, /©S V Lumagraphica for p47, /©Triggerphoto for p48(a), /©webphotographeer for p48(b), /©Willie B Thomas for p49(c), /©krzysztof krzyscin for p49(t), /©Norman Chan for p50, /©William Walsh for p53(l), /©Viktor Kitaykin for p63; Masterfile for p66; Masterfile/©Blend Images for p70; Photolibrary/©Image Source for p5, /©Blend Images for p9, /©Superstock for p10(b), /©Comstock for p15(t), /©Comstock for p61(t), /©Radius Images for p73(t), /©Fancy for p77(b), /©Corbis for p78(b); Rex Features for p28(t), 55(t); Rex Features/©20th Century Fox/Everett for p77(cl); Science Photo Library/©Jerry Masson for p55(c), /©David H Hardy for p80(cr); Shutterstock/©Andreas Gradin for p19(1), /©iBird for p19(3), /©Galcka for p19(4), /©Luciano Mortula for p22(c), /©tonobalaguerf for p22(b), /©hfng for p26(c), /©dakolix for p32(cr), /©Debu55y for p42(t), /©Ragnarock for p49(b), /©Tomasz Szymanski for p58, /©Tan Wei Ming for p60(t), /©Semenova Ekaterina for p77(tl), /©minifilm for p77(cr); Travel Adventures.org/©Boris Kester for p20(c).

**Illustrations by** Mark Duffin and Julian Mosedale